travel guide

San Sombrèro

A LAND OF CARNIVALS, COCKTAILS AND COUPS

CHRONICLE BOOKS

SAN FRANCISCO

www.jetlag.com

Hardie Grant Books
85 High Street
Prahran Victoria 3181
Australia
www.hardiegrant.com.au

Distributed in Canada by Raincoast Books
9050 Shaughnessy Street
Vancouver, British Columbia V6P 6E5

10 9 8 7 6 5 4 3 2 1

Chronicle Books LLC
85 Second Street
San Francisco, CA 94105
www.chroniclebooks.com

Pelvo!

[Welcome!]

Written by Santo Cilauro, Tom Gleisner & Rob Sitch
Edited by Martine Lleonart
Design by Trisha Garner
Maps by Bruce McGurty and Zed Senbergs
Printed and bound in China by SNP Leefung

PHOTOGRAPHY
Jess Bialek 29, 118/119, 125, 140/141, 146 **Michèle Burch** 7, 24, 36, 70, 75, 86,
170, 194, 198 **Ian Burch** 197, 198, 199 **Carole Burch** 197 **Melinda Dillon** 194
Trisha Garner 121 **Hwa Goh** 41, 82, 130, 162 **Adam Haddrick** contents, 49, 54/55,
57, 60, 63, 90/91, 133, 163, 197, 200 **Debra Herman** 7, 8, 9, 32, 38, 58, 72, 77,
88, 120, 159, 176, 191 **Fiona Herman** 64 **Freda Hirsh** contents, 18, 19, 25, 46, 52,
79, 118/119, 136, 144, 147, 155, 189 **Neno Mariani** 62, 120 **Paul Mercer** 69, 124
Marty Rudolph 196 **Emmanuel Santos** 96, 12 **Angela Sutton** 30, 44, 54/55
Mark Vickers-Willis contents, 24, 28, 29, 47, 48, 53, 66, 93, 94, 113, 114, 118/119,
134, 139, 156, 158, 165, 170, 182/183, 184, 185, 186 **Working Dog** (Santo Cilauro,
Tom Gleisner, Rob Sitch) welcome, contents, 8, 12, 14-22, 24, 27–36, 38, 40–46, 48–52,
54/55, 58–61, 63–75, 77–85, 87–94, 96–103, 105, 107, 109, 111–117, 120, 123,
124, 126, 128, 131, 132, 134, 136, 137, 138, 140/141, 142, 143, 145, 146,
148, 149–152, 154, 155, 157–171, 173, 174, 175, 177–181, 184–191, 194, 196
istockphoto.com 147

GRAPHICS
Milo Angel 54/55, 56, 57, 63, 86, 121 **Michèle Burch** 11, 86, 121 **Trisha Garner** 37
Guy Holt inside flap,85

ILLUSTRATIONS
Michèle Burch 104, 133 **Bettina Guthridge** 18, 21, 23, 137, 146

COVER PHOTOGRAPHY
Adam Haddrick main portrait, dancers **Working Dog** background to portrait

HOT GUIDE PHOTOGRAPHY
Getty Images cover, inside cover **istockphoto.com** cover,2,3,4,5,6,7,9,10,11,13,14,17,
18,19,20,23,24,25,26,27, back cover **shutterstock.com** 9,12,14,15,16,18,21,22,28
Michael Hirsh 8 **Nic Kocher** 10,19

THE AUTHORS WOULD LIKE TO THANK:
Christian Argenti, Daniel Atkins, The Bulleen Zebras Soccer Club and Juventas old Boys,
Carole Burch, Ian Burch, Michèle Burch, Mandy Carter, CELAS, Kim Choate, Jasmin Chua,
Melinda Dillon, Jon Fothergill, Trisha Garner, Nilson Gomez, Sandy Grant, Sue Hadwen,
Shane Hammond, Hardie Grant Books, Rose Hawas, David Herman, Debra Herman,
Fiona Herman, Freda Hirsh, Will Houghton QC, Nic Kocher, James Liotta, Sebastian Liotta,
Paul Mercer, Tracey Prince, Ulrich Prince, Greg Sitch, Stathi Konstantopoulos, James O'Connor,
Dale Smith, Matt Stewart, Angela Sutton, Don Taylor, Trinidad Wallace, Lisa Wang

Contents

How to Use This Guide

Jetlag Guides are designed to help you get the most out of a country. They provide detailed practical information, a list of 'must-see' attractions and a region-by-region breakdown of every area covered. In the event of an emergency, the final 20 pages are always edible.

Jetlag Travel Guides are broken up into sections, called 'chapters', each one made up of 'pages' covered with 'words' that, when read from left to right, form 'sentences' containing useful tips, cultural information, travel highlights and, more often than not, verbs.

ABOUT THIS BOOK

All Jetlag Guides are printed on quality Polymat™ paper, guaranteed not to crumple, tear, smudge or dissolve in water. Due to its uniquely unstable chemical composition certain pages may, however, burst into flame upon contact with oxygen.

SYMBOLS

Throughout this guide the following symbols are used:

★★★★   Absolutely not to be missed

★★★   Well worth a visit

★★   If you're in the area and have some spare time

💣   Avoid

The following methods of payment are accepted:

V   Visa

AE   American Express

C/C   Cash or cigarettes

CODE OF CONDUCT

Jetlag writers do not accept discounts or payments in exchange for positive coverage. That said, they are willing to overlook a hotel or restaurant's minor deficiencies in return for a small 'fee', sent care of the publisher.

Contributors

Raoul Mykal was given responsibility for compiling our section on San Sombrèro's modern political history, spending many months in the country researching both government and military activities. He has not been heard of in eight months and his contribution is published here, we can only assume, posthumously.

Graham Thorne is a palaeontologist with a special interest in Latin American civilisation. David has spent the last eleven years studying pre-Mayan iconography, Aztec mythology and Incan burial rituals. He would really like a girlfriend.

Salina Haines is an expert on travel health and has personally been stricken with giardia, dysentery, cholera, yellow fever and just about every other form of gastro-intestinal ailment known to medical science. She wrote the chapter on Staying Healthy, in between trips to the bathroom.

David Sudderton arrived at the Jetlag offices in 2001, describing himself as a sociologist, anthropologist and linguist. A subsequent check of his resume revealed he was, in fact, a courier, but by then he'd already been given a desk and turned out to be quite good at maps.

Justac van der Kllinffhooven was supposed to draw the maps but ended up doing little more than steal stationery supplies, claim taxi vouchers and complain that no-one could pronounce his surname. He is only included as a contributor in return for dropping his unfair dismissal claim.

Dawn Poynter joined Jetlag as a trainee designer, and went on to become assistant editor before leaving us suddenly to start her own publishing company, an ill-conceived venture that failed spectacularly, taking down not only herself, but a string of investors (many of whom were family members). She then came crawling back and was given a windowless office along with the painstaking task of compiling the hotel listings for this guide. Welcome back, Dawn!

Feature Contributors

As always, Jetlag Guides strives to bring its readers the very latest in travel tips and trends. In this edition we are pleased to offer specialist commentary from…

HELENA DDØRK
Eco-Tourism Expert

Helena actually began her travels late in life, refusing to leave home until issued with a passport printed on recycled paper using non-toxic ink produced, where possible, by indigenous cooperatives. But she's more than made up for this late start by tirelessly researching and campaigning for environmentally responsible tourism. A regular contributor to publications such as *Clean, Green & Smug* and author of *Southeast Asia on Less Than One Carbon Credit*, her message to anyone visiting a foreign land is as simple as it is practical…

'Tread carefully, and leave nothing but footprints, unless you're crossing a fragile mountain grass plateau, in which case don't tread at all but consider hovering above the ground in a hot air balloon.'

COREY WATTS
Adventure Travel

The story goes that Corey was actually dropped as a baby, his fall only broken by the umbilical cord stretching tight, unofficially making him the youngest -ever bungee jumper. Corey's love of adventure and extreme sports travel has seen him bicycle, canoe, raft, sled, kayak, glide and climb his way round the world, in between lengthy hospital stays and insurance claims. He is the first person to have successfully jet-boated through the canals of Venice and is currently in training to jump the Great Wall of China on a dirt bike. Corey's philosophy on travel is clear…

'Why settle for a cultural experience when you can have a near-death one?'

TINA PAYNE
Safety First

The day Tina first left home with a kevlar money belt double-padlocked to her waist, she developed a love of adventurous travel, tempered with an overwhelming sense of its inherent dangers. Since then she's been lost, over-charged, swindled, ripped-off and robbed in over a dozen countries, all of which incidents form the basis for her autobiography, *Passport to Fear*. When not warily roaming the globe, Tina chairs a Fretful Travellers self-help group.

'Beware of anyone who is friendly or polite – chances are they're targeting you for a scam.'

PHILIPPE MISEREE
Professional Traveller

As a four-year-old boy, Philippe wandered off from his parent's country home and spent almost a week staggering around in cold, wet conditions, completely alone and lost. For him, it was the start of a love affair with serious travel that has lasted a lifetime. Philippe divides travellers into two groups: superficial tourists too frightened to venture off the beaten path or leave the mental comfort of their narrow-minded world viewpoint, and himself.*

'If your overseas trip is not arduous and, at times, distressingly uncomfortable – then you run the very serious risk of it turning into a holiday.'

* For more information about Philippe, visit his new website **www.beenthereb4u.com**

Thank you!

Many thanks to the travellers who used our last edition and wrote to us with helpful hints, advice and interesting anecdotes. These are much appreciated.

However, correspondence involving lengthy and detailed descriptions of your sexual conquests abroad (even if they *did* take place at cultural sites) have no value or place in a modern travel guide such as this. We respectfully request that readers cease sending this sort of information and, more specifically, the photographic attachments.

Fully Updated!

Thanks to reader feedback, coupled with the mysterious disappearance of our supervising editor, this latest edition of *San Sombrèro* has been extensively revised and fully updated.

Correction. In our last edition we noted that the hill town of Miguela was a good place to buy rugs. It is, in fact, a good place to buy drugs. We apologise to any residents who may have taken offence.

Disclaimer

While every attempt has been made to ensure this guide to San Sombrèro is accurate and up-to-date, remember that Central America is a volatile part of the world where things often change. Governments fall, currencies are devalued, pristine rainforests disappear – all often on a weekly basis. If you do spot an error or omission in this guide, please let us know. The best letters or emails will receive a free copy of our next edition. The most critical or insulting correspondence will be passed on to our defamation lawyers.

WHAT'S IN A NAME?

The full and technically correct name of San Sombrèro is, of course, the Democratic Free People's United Republic of San Sombrèro. (Failure to use this official title may, under certain circumstances, result in citizens being arrested without a warrant.) However, in the interests of brevity we have chosen to use the simpler, shortened version of San Sombrèro throughout this guide.

Ministero de Turismo de San Sombrèro

Casa Provincial
254 Avenida Jurgez
Armadillion
Cucaracha City

Greetings your friend!

The territory of San Sombrero are without doubt undoubtedly
wealthy in her traditions, culture, religion and idiosyncrasy
unique and prominent in the contemporary worlds.

The capital Cucaracha City is the capital and progenitor for
San Sombrero's economy, politics and much beloved National
Government. Here you will found many streets and much
hospitality that irradiates the urban centre whether your stay
is of just one day or a period greater in duration.

San Sombrero is eagerly desired by beach-lovers who come in
translucent bathing costumes to enjoy the pleasure of our
virgins white sand and temperate waters populated by
multicoloured fishes and blue sky where flying sea gulls fly
to welcome you with their flight.

If you like to have the adventure of discovery then much in
San Sombrero awaits to excite you. Elevated mountains and
jungle-clad jungles are just two examples of a multifarious
list trifling with delights.

All over San Sombrero your soul will be tickled by numerous
natural jewels owing to the unique topography and cultural
richness of the region. An imperious experience awaits the
lover of ancient times and art. Or you may simple choose to
choose to stay and enjoy the healthful beaches combined with
reposeful hotels that boast of excellent servitude and will
prove it to be.

The people of San Sombrero are be your willing hosts and with
whom you will share many precious intimacies which will not
only entertain but pleasure you all over.

Whoever you choose to do in San Sombrero, I wish you.

Mr A. J. Mazzora
Ministro de Turismo

Note: *Since writing this letter Mr Mazzora has given up his position as Minister for Tourism portfolio to pursue personal business interests. He is now San Sombrèro's Finance Minister.*

Many visiting photographers agree that the best time to capture San Sombrèro's beauty is early morning; not only is the light good, they are less likely to have their camera stolen.

A Portrait of San Sombrèro

How does one begin to sum up a country like San Sombrèro? 'Beguiling'? 'Vibrant'? 'A magical mix of modern-day charm and **old world** epidemics'? Of course, it is all these things – and more – making this sun-drenched republic one of the most **exciting travel destinations** in all of Central America. Whilst small, this action-and attraction-packed country draws thousands of visitors each year, lured by its tropical charms, exotic lifestyle and lack of extradition treaties with the Western world.

So Much to Do

From the frenetic nightlife of its capital, Cucaracha City, to the guaranteed solitude of a west coast beach during **sea-snake** season, there's simply so much to see and do in this exotic, tropical jewel.

More than anything else, San Sombrèro is a land of **fascinating contradictions**, where Catholic churches permit animal sacrifices, and school canteens sell rum. Its people, too, are an **intriguing mix**, making it little wonder that San Sombrèro boasts the only Nobel Peace Prize winner to ever be accused of war crimes.

Straddling the azure waters of the Caribbean and Pacific, San Sombrèro's first **foreign visitor** was Jorge Paradoure, Spain's most **short-sighted** explorer who confidently identified the land mass as China before stepping ashore and planting a Spanish flag into his own foot (for more, see History section). The country was then colonised and the influence of **Spain** on the San Sombrèran people remains strong to this day, in their language, cuisine and fundamental inability to be anywhere on time.

Something for Everyone

Despite its relatively small size, San Sombrèro offers so many options. Its capital is home to one of the world's largest **Latin music festivals**, and organisers boast that each year almost ten thousand people turn up for the event, partly making up for the fifty odd thousand who routinely flee the city.

Then there's **historic centres**, such as the colonial settlement of Fumarolé, home to the magnificently preserved **Presidential Palace** where, on weekends, visitors might be lucky enough to catch a glimpse of brightly dressed **State Guards** driving military vehicles round the parade grounds while letting off **firearms**; this is not an official display – they're generally just drunk.

Further afield in the mountain hamlet of Cohlera you'll find the stately **cathedral** of San Pedro, noted for its massive **organ**, as was he.

And for those wanting to simply relax, head for the dazzling off-white sands of resort cities such as Playa Miguel, where the **adventurous traveller** can catch a wave, a fish, a hot band and dengue fever all in the one day.

Dirty Dancing!

Of course, no introduction to San Sombrèro would be complete without reference to the country's passion for **song** and **dance**. The traditional music of San Sombrèro is considered to be as **infectious** as many of the nation's water-borne diseases and, as for dancing, it doesn't get much **hotter** than the *bababumba*, the national dance of San Sombrèro. Similar to a rumba, the *bababumba* enacts a breezy battle between a man and a woman who tries to parry his **insistent advances**. Truth be told, this dance is a thinly disguised simulation of the **sexual act** and will generally end in a passionate embrace followed, in many cases, by pregnancy.

Beautiful People

But more than anything else, it is the **people** of San Sombrèro who many regard as the 'main' attraction, and first-time visitors are invariably struck by the natural **beauty** of its citizens. This is a country where ugliness (or '*aranche*') is officially classified as a **disability** and even prisoners have **solarium rights**. The San Sombrèran women, in particular, proudly flaunt their looks and sexuality, with baby girls often learning to **shimmy** before they can walk. And, despite moves to ban the practice, female **soldiers** serving in San Sombrèran **regiments** frequently disobey orders by re-designing their combat uniforms to create a bare midriff.

SEX IN THE CITY

Whether it's the steamy climate, Latin passion or a fundamental lack of self-control, San Sombrèrans certainly can't seem to keep their hands off each other, and on just about every street corner you'll see couples in passionate embrace, whether they're lovers, a married couple or just someone asking for directions.

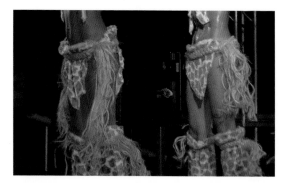

Female members of San Sombrèro's armed forces model their latest camouflage uniforms.

San Sombrèran marching bands often play in public parks to entertain visitors and frighten off unwanted fruit bats.

Trouble in Paradise

Of course, San Sombrèro is not a country without its problems. Political **instability** has seen 17 different **presidents** take power in the past decade, the shortest reign being that of Alivio Escrevez who was **assassinated** halfway through his own inauguration speech.*

The economy, too, continues to struggle with recessions, depressions, de-valuations and **financial crises** regularly plaguing the country. Of course, San Sombrèro's struggle for economic buoyancy has not been helped by the fact its people observe 362 separate **public holidays** (not counting the *carnivale* long weekend). But it's not all gloom. A recent campaign to wipe out illiteracy has enjoyed **great success**, with over 53,000 citizens who were unable to read having now been jailed or deported to Haiti.

But for all its political and economic reforms, San Sombrèro remains a **Third World** country, one in which **tourism** plays a massively important role. Here taxi drivers earn more than doctors (though neither require formal qualifications) and new hotels open up just as quickly as the **building inspectors** can be bought off.

* His assailant was later identified as the Chief Justice who was officiating at the swearing-in ceremony and who himself went on to become president.

01 San Sombrèro
GETTING STARTED

History

Before the arrival of the Spanish, San Sombrèro was known to be inhabited by numerous Amer-Indian **ethnic groups**, such as the *Siboney*, who were nomadic hunters-gatherers, the **coastal-dwelling** *Taino*, who lived on seafood, the *Puorcina*, who practised simple agriculture and the most dominant group, the *Guanajaxo*, a nomadic tribe who simply roamed about **stealing** from everyone else.

Many Bollivquar people remain heavy smokers, such as this teenager, seen here wearing a distinctive hat, or **sombrefuego***, which doubles as an ashtray.*

But the earliest known people, pre-dating all other **tribes** by some five hundred years, were the *Bollivquar*, **fierce warriors** who regarded themselves as a complex, highly **advanced society** – a view somewhat at odds with the fact that they never quite mastered fire, irrigation or star jumps. They did, however, learn to cultivate *cohiba* (tobacco), which formed a large part of their **diet**, perhaps explaining the people's unusually stunted growth.

Life for the *Bollivquar* was governed by the **simple rules** of survival. Each day the **resourceful women** of the tribe would go out and gather fruits, seeds and grain from surrounding **forests**. They would then come back and sell this produce to the men.

BOOK NOTE!
The Ancient Bollivquar by anthropologist Robert J Huston is considered the definitive text on this fascinating tribe. The first half deals with the indigenous people's story chronologically and discusses various aspects of their culture. The second chronicles Professor Huston's relationship with a 16-year-old descendant of a native chief and, while less academically esteemed, is rumoured to be the subject of an upcoming US telemovie.

One of the most useful tools for gauging the sophistication of a civilisation is the stone point, as its development reflects technological advances. Above are several 10th century attempts by Bollivquar tribes-people at creating a hunting spear. (Whilst largely unsuccessful, these designs did lead to the invention of the nacho.)

In the north of San Sombrèro lived another tribe, the *Ciboneque*, who probably arrived from the **Orinoco Basin** sometime during the 8th century. The *Ciboneque* were largely **hunter-gatherers**, although several later developed into **gatherer-hunters** while a small sub-group did neither, preferring to steal and horde.

FASCINATING FACT
The *Ciboneque* reached their artistic, scientific and architectural peak sometime around AD 1000, their decline roughly coinciding with the invention of the hammock.

As the *Ciboneque* drifted south they entered lowland forest territory belonging to the *Parcincqua* people, and it wasn't long before these two **tribes** were rubbing shoulders. Truth be known, they must have rubbed more than just shoulders as, over the coming years, **inter-breeding** took place at a furious rate.

Built during the 9th century, the magnificent ruins at Colloquarva were used each year by various tribes who would come for several weeks of feasting, drinking and ceremonies. As such, these buildings are believed to be the first ever example of a time-share resort.

Spanish Discovery

For the indigenous people of San Sombrèro, life changed forever in September 1502, when **Jorge Paradoure**, thinking he had discovered the Atlantic route to the Orient, ran aground on a small island off the eastern coast of the country. The **legendary explorer** immediately did two things – claim the land for Spain, and sack his navigator.

The Conquistadors

It didn't take long for news of this distant **discovery** to reach Spain and conquest of the country began soon after. In 1506 Captain Don Diegos Estremoz arrived, coming **ashore** just north of present day Vallanca with a heavily-armed landing party. Native **resistance** was minimal, limited to just a few **skirmishes** and a strongly worded smoke-signal.

The next foreigner to attempt a landing was **Alfonso Diaz**, as ruthless a leader as any in San Sombrèran history. Diaz arrived in 1507 with four ships carrying 300 settlers, along with his **buxom** wife Maria who had been brought along as **ballast**.

An impetuous figure, upon arrival Diaz burnt his expedition's boats, to ensure that none of the **crew** tried leaving. Due to a break down in **communication**, however, many of his crew were on board the boats at the time, and subsequently perished.

With his remaining conquistadors, Diaz set about building a **settlement** on the lush shores of what is now known as Ricosta Bay. Once again, the Spanish **settlers** were greeted with friendliness by indigenous tribes of the area, who gave them a rare form of **pink orchid** (left). In return, the Spanish gave them a rare form of gonorrhea.

Government

The first official governor of San Sombrèro was Estrillio Vellasquez, a man who left a lasting **legacy** on the new colony, mainly in the form of illegitimate children.

The Spanish invaders were, ostensibly, charged with **converting** the country's native population to **Christianity**. But gold and silver were their real objectives, and it wasn't long before most Indians were enslaved in mines.

However, the Spanish found little gold or **precious metals** in San Sombrèro and Governor Vellasquez was forced to find another means of generating **wealth** from the colony. Looking around at the **lush vegetation**, rich volcanic soils and tropical climate, to him the answer appeared obvious – a golf course. But before work on this project could begin the order came from **Spain** that San Sombrèro was to start producing **sugar**. Within months entire forests were felled and numerous plantations established.

Sugar

Whilst the **sugar crops** thrived, by this stage San Sombrèro was facing a serious lack of manual labour. During the first **decade** of European settlement thousands of Native Americans had been killed, either in battle or from exposure to **viruses** the Spaniards brought with them, such as smallpox, tuberculosis and a particularly **aggressive** form of tinea.

Surviving members of the country's indigenous **population** were forced to labour on various **plantations** but as by this stage there were only 17 left, it proved impossible to fully manage the workload.

Slavery

As the production levels of San Sombrèran **sugar** grew during the 1520s the country's economy expanded, as did the average national dress size. Too **fat** to work on the plantations themselves, large numbers of *melleco* people from western Africa were brought across as **slave labourers**. Of course, San Sombrèro's sugar **crops** are no longer harvested by slaves – desperate backpackers now do most of the the the heavy work.

The historic Castillo del Almas *has survived centuries of armed attack, its outer wall having only ever been breached once by a German cruise ship that sailed into it during a night of heavy fog and even heavier drinking.*

Piracy

In addition to sugar, by the second half of the 16th century San Sombrèro was also producing coffee, tobacco, **rubber** and a large range of **tropical fruits**. However, getting this produce safely out of the country became increasingly difficult with a rise in **piracy** seeing Italian, English, Dutch and Portuguese buccaneers all plying the nearby seas.

At one point there were so many pirates sailing offshore that an entire industry developed manufacturing **eye-patches**. Despite the formation of a defence alliance, FAPN (**Federated Association of Plundered Nations**), in 1548, attacks on San Sombrèran ships continued at an alarming rate.

And it wasn't just her ships – Cucaracha City itself was raided by **pirate gangs** on numerous occasions. So audacious were these seagoing **scoundrels** that on one occasion in 1562 Henry Maddock, a stocky Welshman and leader of the Buccaneers, sailed into Cucaracha City's **harbour** and brazenly made off with the Governor's wife. The fact she went **willingly** only added further insult to Spanish pride.

FASCINATING FACT

During the 16th century the sea off San Sombrèro was so crowded with pirate ships that sailors forced to 'walk the plank' would often find themselves falling into another boat.

Attempts at defending early settlements by building heavily fortified castles proved of limited success, in part due to the fact that many of the canons turned out to be purely decorative.

'LA DIABLA'

Of all the pirates who plied their trade off the coast of San Sombrèro during the 17th century, it was a woman who most struck fear into the hearts of honest sailors.

Isobel Alvarra was born in Lisbon in 1597, the daughter of wealthy merchants. As a young girl she yearned to become a sailor but her parents refused, saying a life at sea was not for young ladies. When Isobel cut off her long hair in protest, her mother and father were unmoved. When she grew a thick beard they realised she was serious and relented.

Rejected by merchant ships (it was considered bad luck to have a woman on board), Isobel disguised herself as a man and joined the crew of a pirate vessel headed for the Caribbean. She stayed in this guise for many months and was said to have been as fierce and dangerous as any man (especially when pre-menstrual) and no-one questioned her. Had it not been for her habit of sunbathing topless, Isobel's cover might never have been blown. But so skilled was she with pistol and rapier (not to mention a pastry brush) that, instead of being thrown overboard, Isobel was appointed captain, leading her crew on a series of daring attacks.

Known as La Diabla ('the Devil Woman'), she was often moody and soon developed a reputation for having a fiery temper, once thrashing a young crew member for making sexual advances, and another for failing to do so.

Spanish authorities grew increasingly concerned about her activities and, in 1634, sent a large fleet to capture the brazen buccaneer. Surrounded and greatly outnumbered, Isobel was ordered to give up but 'surrender' was not a word in her vocabulary (she only spoke Portuguese). Instead, she outran the armada and continued to plunder ships and towns along the San Sombrèran coast.

By this time Isobel was married to Jake O'Meare, an Irish pirate, and discovered she was pregnant but managed to keep her condition secret for many months by claiming to be carrying a spare cannonball. Eventually the couple were forced ashore where Isobel gave birth to an almost healthy boy (he was born with a peg-leg).

Before she could return to sea, Spanish authorities arrested Isobel and she was sentenced to death. But the Governor of San Sombrèro stepped in and said 'I will not allow a woman to hang'. The following day Isobel was beheaded.

One of the most daring, brutal and ruthless of all San Sombrèro's pirates, in 1647 Isobel Alvarra became the first female ever to be inducted into the Buccaneer's Hall of Fame.

The Struggle for Independence

By the beginning of 19th century, Spain's status as **world power** was in decline and its hold over San Sombrèro slowly became weakened. But the colony was still valuable to **Spain** and any mention of 'independence' was brutally suppressed. Nevertheless, the **independence movement** continued to gain steam, prompting Governor Manuel Cespedes to change tack.

In 1804 he invited all interested parties - whether they were reformists, independence campaigners or intellectuals – to Cucaracha City for a **convention** on future self-rule. He listened to their arguments for three days and then had them all imprisoned without trial for 27 years.

Economically, San Sombrèro continued to **struggle**. As sugar prices dropped during the early 19th century, other **crops** were introduced such as coffee and bananas, the latter actually becoming San Sombrèro's **official currency** for several decades.

Bananas, coconuts and, for a short period, cigars, have all been used as legal tender.

Patriot Priest

One of the earliest and most famous leaders of San Sombrèro's **independence movement** was Creole priest Padre Miguel Hostilla, who issued his famous cry 'San Sombrèro Libre!' from the steps of his parish church on 17 October 1809. A small group of **citizens** gathered below simply assumed Hostilla was drunk again (he was wearing no pants at the time) and ignored this cry but the **determined priest** refused to be silenced.

He organised a campaign of civil disobedience and assembled a group of **freedom fighters** who attempted to capture Government House in Cucaracha City. On 12 December over 1000 **heavily armed** men surrounded the building. Before attacking, Father Hostilla inspired the mob with a rousing speech, although the sight of their leader then delivering himself the **Last Rites** did not exactly fill the men with confidence. The **bid** failed and Hostilla was arrested and condemned to be hung, drawn, quartered and then burnt at the stake. However, thanks to **last-minute** plea bargaining, he was given 8 million hours of community service.

Independence at Last

Despite attempts by Spanish authorities to stifle the **independence movement**, by the end of the 19th century it was obvious their days as rulers were numbered.

In 1892, a **massive rally** on the foreshore in Cucaracha City saw 120,000 protestors assemble, calling for freedom of expression, universal suffrage and property rights. After **several hours** of drinking and eating, public toilets were added to their list of demands. The rally was addressed by **local author** Ingo Cadiz who decided to galvanize the crowd by reading one of his **lengthy poems**. This recitation had the desired effect; the crowd united against Cadiz and threw him into the **harbour**. Fired up, they then continued on to Government House, over-running its now-depleted **defences** and taking control.

At 4.30pm on the afternoon of 8 September, the Spanish flag was torn down and replaced by a stained red-and-white checked **tablecloth**, the interim flag of San Sombrèro. An independent nation at last!

Democracy

San Sombrèro was declared a **democratic republic**, presided over by a constitutional assembly and 80-member directly elected parliament. This structure lasted three days before San Sombrèro's newly appointed **armed forces** head General Pablo Veracruz (himself a former freedom fighter) seized control, imprisoning the assembly, dismissing the **parliament** and declaring himself Supreme Ruler. This event is often referred to by San Sombrèran historians as the 'stillbirth of the nation'.

Totalitarianism

From this time on San Sombrèro's military have had a constant **involvement** in the country's politics, so much so that even today **Question Time** in parliament is often referred to as **Interrogation Time**.

Veracruz ruled for almost a decade – now considered quite long in San Sombrèran terms. Due to the **volatility** of its people, coupled with a lack of **gun control**, the average presidential term is barely three months.

President Veracruz was succeeded by President Alonso Raiban, a deeply **unpopular leader** who ruled, not only with the aid of a secret police force, but also a secret fire brigade. He was followed by President Pepe Sapique whose four-year **tenure** was marked by corruption, the abolition of all civil rights and a massive economic downturn. Disturbingly, this period is considered something of a '**Golden Age**' for 20th century San Sombrèro.

In the San Sombrèran police force rank is generally designated by the length of braiding on an officer's trousers.

Recent Years

1970s

The past few decades have not been easy for San Sombrèro. During the 1970s the country was hit by **hyperinflation**. The government attempted to pull out of this economic malaise by diversifying the economy, which had long been **dominated** by coffee and bananas. In 1975 San Sombrèro announced plans to produce banana-flavoured coffee, an **initiative** that met with limited export success.

1980s

In an effort to kick-start the **economy** during the 1980s, President Javier Fulvares embarked on series of major capital works, however – as most involved improvements to his **family beach house** and connecting roads – these had little long-term fiscal benefit. President Fulvares was deposed in 1984 by his half brother Jose whose six-month term was marked by ultra-conservatism, corruption and **repression**. He did, however, introduce **compulsory seat belts**, for which he was presented with a humanitarian award.

Tainted by constant accusations of corruption, Fulvares agreed to leave **office**, only to be replaced by a man who looked disarmingly **identical**, except for a bad wig and drawn-on moustache. The **scam** worked for a few months but eventually the stand-in leader was given the honour reserved for all deposed leaders, a 21-gun **salute** – from a firing squad.

1990s

Another crisis rocked the country in 1992 when a shortage of **gold** meant several San Sombrèran generals were left without sufficient embroidery on their caps. The following year one of these **disgruntled** leaders, General Miguella (known as *'El Bolle'* for his choice of ever-present sunglasses), seized **power**. Miguella had received much of his education at the Fumarolé Military School where he excelled in physics, **history** and suppression.

President Miguella took power promising to construct schools, **highways** and a health care system. However, he was a uniquely corrupt man, susceptible to *la mordida* (literally, the bite – bribes) and only clung to **power** through a personal **police force** of 15,000. Several attempts were made on his life (mainly by his immediate family) and **public unrest** threatened to boil over. Eventually the sadistic and psychopathic leader was forced to flee the country and is now living in South America where he is best known as the **nasty judge** on TV's *Peruvian Idol.*

Since then San Sombrèro has been ruled by a total of 12 presidents, president-elects, **interim presidents** and a high-school student doing work experience.

Members of San Sombrèro's indigenous tribes will often visit town to trade food, animal hides, beads and – more recently – foreign currency.

The People

The population of San Sombrèro is said to be 8.6 million although this figure is **approximate** as no thorough formal **census** has ever been conducted. To gauge family sizes, officials will often just count the number of people **lounging** in a doorway – and multiply by 11.

San Sombrèro's **family-planning** policies have helped reduce its **birth rate**, as did the introduction of cable TV in the mid-90s. However, teenage pregnancies continue to be a problem and in recent years people have become so **promiscuous** that their behaviour has actually sparked the country's second rubber boom.

San Sombrèro's most recent **census** reports that, officially, about 55% of its **population** is white, mainly of Spanish origin. About 14% is black and 23% *mulattoes* of **mixed ethnicity**. The remainder are CIA operatives.

Over the centuries each of these **groups** have intermingled, producing a fascinating – if sometimes volatile – **national identity**. Remarkably, there is very little in the way of racial tension in San Sombrèro, with blacks, whites and those of **mixed race** all happily living, working and stealing from each other.

Eternally **patient**, San Sombrèrans are willing to queue for hours to be allowed into a queue that will give them access to another **queue** to buy a ticket for a bus that may never come and if it does will be late and going the **wrong** way. Of course, for them – philosophically – it's not a 'queue' – it's the start of a conga line.

The people of San Sombrèro are generally outgoing, **talkative** and sociable, which perhaps **explains** why so few have succeeded as spies.

Whether it's the languid tropical heat or the rum-based breakfast **cereals** so widely enjoyed, nothing seems to happen in a hurry here. People laze in their doorways, or stop mid-sentence for a nap. So **laid-back** are many San Sombrèrans that last year the city's inaugural **marathon** had to be abandoned when, several hours after the official start, most of the field were still chatting, while even the most eager of **competitors** made it no further than the first drinks station.

Above all else, San Sombrèrans are **happy** people. For them, smiling comes naturally and it's not unusual to see large groups of people, doubled over with **laughter** and merriment, even after **car crashes**. The ability to see the lighter side of hardship or tragedy is a unique feature of San Sombrèran life, making it one of the few countries where **anti-depressant** medication is virtually unheard of.

So content are most San Sombrèrans that smiling is almost considered a national pastime. In fact, frowning on public holidays will attract a fine.

Customs & Traditions

San Sombrèrans love to **celebrate** and each stage of their lives is marked with great tradition and ceremony.

Birth

A truly **joyous event**, always attended by the husband and, where possible, father of the child.

Turning 15

A direct legacy of their Spanish heritage, *Las fiestas de quince* represents a special **birthday** party for 15-year-old girls. Parents will save money from the day their daughter is born in order to create a **memorable** occasion. It's the day on which she may openly begin her sexual life without societal **recrimination** or having to use the family car. The event is usually marked by **mass** during which the girl receives Holy Communion and her first cell phone.

Weddings

In San Sombrèro people can **marry** at 16 (or 14 with their parents' consent and/or credit card).

Divorce

Sadly, San Sombrèro suffers from an alarmingly high **divorce** rate, with many of its people having been married three times, often in the one week. Worried by this **trend**, the president of San Sombrèro recently declared 2005 'Year of the Family', with a special **Marriage Taskforce**, headed by two of his former wives.

Funerals

San Sombrèrans treat death in the same way they treat most events – as an **excuse** for a party. When a **senior** family member dies their relatives will dress in black and a sign will be placed outside the home reading *casa muerte* ('room for rent').

BIRTHDAY BASH!
At any child's birthday celebration you are likely to see the young guests, gathered round a candy-filled effigy, or *piñata*, hanging from a tree. Blindfolded participants take turns swinging long sticks at this figurine, all hoping to smash it open. In many San Sombrèran jails confessions are extracted from political prisoners in much the same way.

Education

In 1927 one of San Sombrèro's greatest presidents and man of letters, General Morello, declared 'the only way to be free is to be educated'. Why he then proceeded to close **schools** and burn public **libraries** remains an enduring **enigma**, but this belief in the importance of education remains **strong** to this day.

A typical school day begins with the singing of the national **anthem**, followed by reading of patriotic books, mathematics, dancing, flirting and then a **siesta** before everyone heads off to a nightclub.

San Sombrèro is justifiably **proud** of its educational system and actively encourages **intellectual** discourse. Debating competitions are always exciting (especially those involving hand-to-hand **combat**) and even the most **remote** village has its own school. Music and dance plays such a fundamental role in schooling that in some classes the teacher sits at a **mixing desk**.

San Sombrèro's school buses break down with such frequency that in 2001 it was decided that classes would now be held on board these vehicles.

Women & Machismo Society

Pretty women walking down the street will often be bombarded with **comments** ranging from *piropos* (witty compliments) to *sleezicos* (straightforward requests for sex). Whilst much of this can be put down to **misplaced** male **machismo**, some of the blame must lie with San Sombrèran women who find it almost impossible not to openly flaunt their **sexuality**.

From the youngest of ages, girls will insist on tight-fitting diapers, before graduating to **high heels** and short skirts. This is, after all, a country that produced the *Borellolites*, the first ever order of **Catholic** nuns to wear habits with a plunging neckline.

Equal Rights

Interestingly, San Sombrèro boasts one of the oldest **feminist** movements in Latin America. As long ago as the 7th century, **indigenous** women of the *Peyonne* tribe demanded – and won – the right to be used as human sacrifices.

San Sombrèro still prides itself on women's rights and has enacted a range of **legislation** to ensure its female population is looked after. Women are guaranteed equal **wages** to men and those workers having a baby are given 10 weeks of paid **maternity leave**. Women trying to conceive are also given time off, along with a collection of massage **oils**, scented candles and a CD of smooth jazz.

Spanish heritage is, of course, **patriarchal**, meaning that the husband has **exclusive rights** to property, finances and, legally, the obedience of his wife and children. After **independence** San Sombrèro replaced this with a new civil code that gave both parties equal rights, although the **husband** did retain exclusive access to the TV remote control.

Tina Writes...
For the Cautious Traveller
Female travellers should be extremely cautious about making eye contact with anyone for longer than a few seconds as this gesture will be considered flirtatious. The only time a woman in San Sombrèro should look directly into a man's eyes is when visiting her optometrist. Even then, be prepared for sexual advances.

> **WHAT'S IN A NAME?**
> San Sombrèran surnames are combinations of the first surname of the person's father, which comes first, and the mother's first surname. Where the identity of the father is unknown, the mother's full name is used, but said with a wink.

A San Sombrèran beauty enjoys some time out with his friend.

Religion

San Sombrèro is officially Catholic, and an independent **survey** recently found that 80% of people had attended **church** in the previous month. In many cases this was purely to steal from the **collection box**, but religion remains an important influence on daily life.

Pre-Christian Beliefs

Of course, well before the Spanish arrived the San Sombrèran people worshipped a variety of gods, including those **deities** they believed to be responsible for the sun, the moon, rain, fire and, curiously, bananas. Many of their **rituals** and ceremonies were dominated by chanting, dancing, human sacrifice and **gratuitous** nudity.

(Left) Dating back at least 1000 years, this votive figure has been described by archaeologists as 'pre-Mayan and post-coital'.

Catholicism

When the Spanish arrived in the early 16th century they set about attempting to convert the native population to **Catholicism**. The concept of a single, **all-powerful** God did not sit well with the locals, who also resisted moves to attend mass, read **scriptures** or even wear pants. They did, however, quite take to **bingo**, and church halls were soon **packed** with eager players.

Religious **imagery** from this period is particularly notable for its rather gory nature, primarily because life for San Sombrèro's **indigenous** people was so hard that early missionaries had to depict the **sufferings** of Christ in exceptionally horrific terms merely in order to make an impression. Hence, **paintings** show Jesus, not only on a cross, but covered in boiling oil with a wild **dog** attached to his one remaining leg.

Similarly, the **Virgin Mary**, so often portrayed standing on the serpent of evil, is – in San Sombrèran **iconography** – generally depicted biting its head off.

Saint Martina Hergez is a much revered figure in San Sombrèro's religious history. In 1684 she established a holy order of nuns dedicated to the ideals of poverty, obedience and mid-week chastity.

Santeria (Afro-Sombrèran Worship)

Santeria, or saint worship, has been deeply entrenched in San Sombrèran culture for 300 years. This **cult** emerged during the slave era when African religious practices were banned as 'pagan'; worshippers simply took their **tribal** gods and dressed them up as **traditional** Catholic figures. Hence, St Peter has horns and a rather long trunk, while the 12 Apostles frequently appear as winged baboons.

A typical Santeria church **ceremony**, with its chanting, body painting and sacrificial rituals, bears little relation to a typical Catholic **ceremony**. About the only obvious common element is that both involve passing round a collection plate.

Afrocathro priests (as they are known) foretell the future using a complex system of **divination** that makes use of stones, seashells, seeds and – more recently – computer modelling. Becoming a **priest** is not easy; aspiring clergy must undergo intense initiation ceremonies, dressing in black and wearing a heavy gold crucifix for an entire year. If a **novitiate** successfully negotiates this period he usually goes on to become either a priest or a rap artist.

Afrocathro is a sensuous religion, lacking the arbitrary moral **restrictions** of Catholicism. The Seven Deadly Sins have been cut back to just **three**, and in terms of formal religious **observance**, it's not technically essential to attend church on Sunday, as long as you drive past one. Given this **relaxed** approach, over the years Afrocathro has attracted legions of **devotees**.

In an effort to woo back members, the **Pope** recently appointed a Papal Delegate to convince the people of San Sombrèro that they should give up drinking, dancing, drugs and free sex in favour of a more **austere** lifestyle. He quit after **two weeks** and is now living in Lambarda with a 21-year-old stripper.

San Sombrèro's Catholic masses feature one of the few forms of liturgical dancing to be routinely performed in a bikini. In fact, dancing is such an integral part of religious services that most churches now have a mirror ball.

MISSIONARIES

In 1757 the Vatican sent a small group of clergymen into the interior – led by the tireless Dom Pedro. Even though there were only eight in all, these priests travelled assiduously from area to area with a large entourage of well-built slave boys. Remarkably, this tiny Catholic order continues to this very day, attempting to do the same work. They are now commonly known as 'friends of Pedro' or 'Pedrophiles'.

Political Structure

- San Sombrèro is classified as a **Totalinocracy**, ruled over by an elected President answerable to a National Assembly of Right Wing Death Squads.

- The President serves a **five-year term** and may only be assassinated by a **two-thirds** majority of parliament.

- San Sombrèro boasts a **bicameral system**, consisting of an Upper House and a Dungeon.

- The National Assembly (*Asemblea Nacional*) is San Sombrèro's supreme **constitutional body** and is vested with ultimate control over the country (however, the Assembly's influence has been greatly **limited** by the fact that, at any given time, most of its 590 members are in exile, in prison or lying in state).

- When the Assembly does meet it is usually to consider **legislation** proposed by the President, which it may chose to either:
  - i) **rubber stamp**,
  - ii) **fast track**, or
  - iii) **pass unanimously** before standing to perform a rousing rendition of the national anthem.

- Ministers are sworn in wearing their traditional **robes** – bulletproof vests.

- After a president **dies** there is an official two-week period of celebration.

> *In 1995 San Sombrèro held its first* **popular election***, characterised by full freedom of the press, frank debates by rival candidates and the threat of* **death** *for anyone who voted against the president. To ensure transparency at the ballot box,* **transparent** *ballot boxes were used, with armed members of the military standing by to assist in* **selecting** *the correct candidate.*

 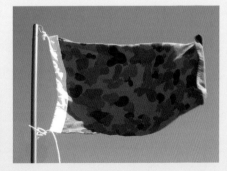

(Left) A cannon strategically placed outside the opposition leader's office provides a constant reminder of his precarious political position. (Right) San Sombrèro's flag is the Camouflagio.

SAN SOMBRERO'S STRUCTURE

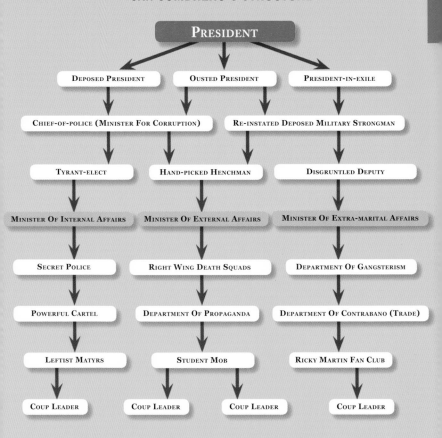

HOW A BILL IS PASSED

STEP 1 – Initiation

The Member of Parliament proposing the legislation presents it for consideration. At this point the Bill's contents are strictly confidential, known only to the Secretary of State and his mistress.

STEP 2 – Processing

After the Secretary of State is satisfied that the Bill contains all the elements necessary for constitutional validity (including $US10,000 in unmarked notes), it is passed onto the Senate Leader. On being handed the document, he utters the traditional words *Que c'e par muno?* ('What's in it for me?').

STEP 3 – Executive Approval

Eventually the Bill is presented to the President who, depending on his reaction, will either execute it or the member who thought it up.

Language

While San Sombrèro is a Spanish speaking country, a peculiar **dialect** has developed, combining elements of Castilian **grammar**, Portuguese pronunciation and indigenous shouting. The biggest **hurdle** facing non-native speakers is that San Sombrèrans speak very fast. In fact, it's regarded as **impolite** to pause for breath during a **sentence**, and this rapid-fire delivery can be somewhat overwhelming, especially if you're speaking to a race-caller or auctioneer.

The good **news** is that you'll find English widely spoken throughout San Sombrèro. It's now required learning for all **university** students as well as anyone in the hospitality trade – most **waiters** will be quite capable of getting your order wrong in a range of languages. Even San Sombrèran kids speak a **smattering** of English although, as much of this is learned from US **hip-hop singers**, be prepared to hear yourself referred to as a 'pimp' or 'skanky ho'. Try not to take offence.

Not surprisingly, many **'Americanisms'** have made their way into the San Sombrèran **vocabulary**. Hence, one goes to watch *besbol*, eats *hamburgesas*, enjoys a few *beeras* and then becomes the **victim** of a *dryvebyshooting*.

Try learning a few words. San Sombrèrans warm quickly to those who make an **effort** to speak their language and you'll be surprised at how quickly you're either **understood** or **arrested** for obscenity. The University of Cucaracha City offers intensive **Spanish language courses** for visitors. Their popular two-week holiday programme – usually includes three to five hours of **instruction**, followed by lectures on culture and history, some group **singing** and a date with the professor of your choice.

English is wildly spoken throughout San Sombrèro.

Philippe Writes... For the Serious Traveller
When overseas I always make the effort to communicate with locals using their own language. Whilst this has, at times, led to confusion, insult and, in 1998, a six-month jail term for inadvertently propositioning a nun, these incidents often make for my most treasured travel memories.

Useful Expressions

Si – Yes

No – No

Buenos dias – Good morning

Buenas tardes – Good afternoon

Buenos noches – Good evening

Buenos nachos – Good nachos

Perdoneme – Excuse me (physical)

Desculpeme – Excuse me (speech)

Olfactoro! – Excuse me (farting)

Disgustia Senora! – Excuse me madam, your penis is showing

NATIONAL ANTHEM

San Sombrèro's national anthem *O Patria Gloriosa* was written in 1853 by independence leader Juan Robirro who, at the age of 22, uttered the famous cry 'he who loves his country lives forever', shortly before falling to his death off a ladder.

It is believed to be one of the only national anthems in the world set to a bossa nova beat. When played, loyal citizens will generally stand and respectfully place one hand on each hip, before starting to gyrate.

San Sombrèrans, while proud of their country, are not overly patriotic as is demonstrated by this first verse.

> *My baby melts my heart*
> *My baby drives me nuts*
> *The way she swings her hips*
> *The way her hair hangs down*
> *Give me a kiss,*
> *Oh gorgeous woman*
> *Cover my lips*
> *In passionate bliss*
> *Long live San Sombrèro*
> *Oh glorious fatherland.*

SPEAK LIKE A NATIVE

Visitors interested in learning to speak San Sombrèran quickly should consider enrolling in one of the many immersion courses offered by various language schools. The most well known of these, Linga Sombrèro, is considered one of the strictest educational institutions in Latin America. Run by Director Colonel Juan Marquez, himself a former military translator, courses here combine traditional methods of learning with modern day techniques of persuasion. Just how effective this approach is tends to be hard to determine, as very few graduating students are prepared to speak openly about their experiences.

There are also numerous books available for those wishing to learn the language, including a series published by Jetlag featuring such popular titles as:

Ola! San Sombrèran
Spanish for beginners

Ole! San Sombrèran
Spanish for bull fighters

Go-o-o-o-o-o-o-o-o-o-ol!
San Sombrèran Spanish for football commentators

Food & Drink

Whilst San Sombrèro may not be the **food-lovers** ultimate destination, it is **possible** to eat well – and cheaply – throughout the country. Traditional San Sombrèran food (*criollo*) takes a range of **culinary influences** – Spanish, African, indigenous – and basically adds coconut. Fish (*pescado*) and **chicken** (*pollo*) are the most common **meats**, closely followed by rabbit (*rodekil*).

In general, San Sombrèrans love their **food** and **nutritionists** will rate every dish for not only its energy value and **fat content**, but also its potential aphrodisiac qualities.

Vegetarians

It's not easy eating **meat-free** in San Sombrèro, as even simple vegetable dishes will often have meat added to 'improve' them. **Rice** and beans are routinely fried in **animal** fat or boiled in stock that has had an animal bone or organ added for extra **flavour**. Even so-called 'vegetarian' restaurants will generally include chicken on the **menu**. If stuck, your best bet is to simply drink **bottled water** (although avoid *Agua Toro* as it may contain small amounts of beef stock).

The most common vegetable is the *platano viando*, a variety of plaintain that is generally **steamed** until tender, a process that can take up to 15 years.

Quick Tip In restaurants, be wary of ordering a 'kids meal' – this will often involve baby goat.

Helena Writes... For the Eco-Traveller

Did you know that disposing of empty plastic water bottles creates enormous environmental problems for developing countries such as San Sombrèro? Consider travelling around with a ceramic gourd, preferably made by local artisans, or lick dew drops from low hanging leaves. Even better still, simply have a large drink before you leave home and thus avoid depleting the community's precious fresh water resources.

Donkey and mule meat is used extensively – especially as an appetizer. This is known locally as 'Hee Haw D'oeuvre'.

Rotulos de huevos is a typical sweet similar to licorice except it is made out of rubber.

Potaje is a thick oily soup made from black beans, with fried garlic, onion, pepper and chilli. It is generally served before a main course or a colonoscopy.

Warning: While the cost of eating out in San Sombrèro is generally quite low, so too are hygiene standards, and diners struck by the sudden onset of gastro-intestinal illness during the middle of a meal may find themselves subject to a 10% 'corkage charge'.

Eating Out

Eating in San Sombrèro is generally **good value** and you can fill up for US$5–10. Admittedly, this will be on beer and corn chips, but at least you won't starve.

When dining out, be **patient**. Service will often take much longer than you're used to at home. In some **instances** it's worth phoning your order in a day or two in advance, more if you're planning on **dessert**. And, while service might be described as 'leisurely', an attempt at sneaking out before paying the bill will, at least. allow you to witness a **crack** display of high-speed security.

In tourist centres, be on guard for rip-offs, often in the form of **phantom** charges such as 'background music fee' or 'use of pepper grinder'. And remember, it is not legal for a restaurant to bill patrons for **dropping serviettes**, leaning back in their chair or failing to leave cutlery in the correct position after a meal.

At San Sombrèran restaurants it is not uncommon for **the waiter** to appear between each course with a brush to clear the table of crumbs and spilt food; this service is more than just a **courtesy**; the scraps collected will generally be used to feed the kitchen staff.

Street Food

A great alternative to formal restaurant dining is the **roadside stall**, selling everything from fried rice to unleaded **fuel** (sometimes in the same bowl). It is here one is likely to taste authentic San Sombrèran **fare**, although some care should be taken in selecting your meal. As a general rule, eat nothing that is **raw**, uncovered or sitting in a box labelled *patología espécimem* ('pathology specimens').

HEY WAITER!
A habit peculiar to Latin American countries such as San Sombrèro is the way waiters are summoned in restaurants. Instead of a discrete wave, local diners will – quite literally – hiss in order to call for service. So if you hear the person at the table next to you let out a loud 'S-s-s-s-s-s', don't be alarmed, they've just called for the bill or, in regional areas, trodden on a snake.

(Clockwise from top) Street vendors in San Sombrèro sell a wide range of food, everything from hot curries, fruit, ice-cream, fried delicacies and lollopo, *a popular children's treat similar to cotton candy except it's made from brightly coloured cocaine.*

Drinks

San Sombrèro's local **mineral water** is *Agua Regurgica*. According to its label this mineral water 'stimulates the digestion' – due, not so much to its **mineral** content, but it's lack of purification.

The most common **soft drink** in San Sombrèro is *Tropico*, a brightly-coloured orange juice. It lacks any real **flavour**, but it's cheap and free of artificial sweeteners, colours and, for that matter, oranges.

San Sombrèro has a fine reputation for its **coffee**; the best place to sample it is Europe, where the majority is **exported**. The local coffee is, unfortunately, often adulterated with other roasted products, such as chicory or coal.

The most widespread and popular drink in San Sombrèro is, of course, **rum**. A part of everyday life in San Sombrèro, rum is a constant **companion** at parties, festivities, weddings and – more often than not – conceptions.

In San Sombrèro a 'Shrimp Cocktail' is, in fact, a drink, made from a mixture of sugar, rum and pureed prawn.

Rum-making begins with the main by-product of **sugar**, molasses, being diluted with water and then fermented with **yeasts**. The resulting **liquid** is then rested, sometimes for up to 12 minutes, in special vats until the right balance of taste, aroma and **combustibility** is obtained. This process is controlled under the guidance of a master **taster** who has both the palate and the liver required for such demanding **duties**. The oldest rum (7–9 years) is drunk neat, while the youngest (5-6 days) is used in lawn mowers.

BOTTOMS UP San Sombrèro is a founding member of the International Cocktail Federation (I.C.F.) and is responsible for a range of exotic mixed drinks, including the **Molotovo** (rum, pineapple, Avgas), the **Inexplicado** (not even the barman knows what's in it) and, of course, the infamous **Toxico,** one of the only beverages in the world to be routinely served with its own antidote. Of course, the country's unofficial cocktail is the **Comatozo** – a fiery mixture of rum, tequila, brandy, Cointreau and a rum top-up followed by a dash of lime (optional). It is most commonly drunk by young people celebrating national holidays or the sick and frail seeking voluntary euthanasia.

Juices (jugos) are also popular, and roadside stalls will often sell a mixed concoction made up of whatever has gone through the extractor, whether it's pineapple, orange, watermelon, lawn clippings or the operator's fingers. San Sombrèro's best fruit and vegetables are generally turned into juices, as is its meat (a 'pork smoothie' being considered a refreshing aperitif).

Music & Dance

Rhythm is **ever-present** in San Sombrèro. From the pulsating beat of a wandering *salsita* band to the **hypnotic thud** of helicopter gun-ships strafing a rebel stronghold, music and dance permeate just about all aspects of **life**. So important is music to San Sombrèrans that, until recently, babies diagnosed as **tone-deaf** were frequently abandoned at birth.

Lack of money or **instruments** has never been a problem as just about anything can be used to make music in San Sombrèro: two pieces of wood, **an empty box**, it's not uncommon to see people on street corners tapping an old **tyre** rim, or prison guards banging inmates' heads together to create a **lively beat**. In general, San Sombrèran music is vibrant and joyful. It's one of the few countries where **funeral marches** often take the form of a samba.

Dance is synonymous with San Sombrèro, and the country has given birth to **many exciting styles**. There's the sensual *grindo*, highly popular as both a **social** dance, and an excellent form of **pelvic** floor exercise. Group routines include the *bombarella*, in which men in Cuban heels stomp on a sombrero – a very **challenging dance**, especially for the person wearing the sombrero.

SOMBRERAN 'TRES'
A small guitar-shaped instrument modelled on the Arab lute. In the 1890s, the top two strings were removed, producing a lighter, sweeter sound. An even more pleasing sound was produced the following decade when all strings were removed and the tres *banged against the ground as a percussion instrument.*

A San Sombrèran policeman uses an accordion to direct traffic.

Of course, it doesn't get much **raunchier** than the steamy *bababumba*. For many years this dance was considered 'working class', on account of its **suggestive hip rolls**, and the fact that it was regularly performed **naked**. The *bababumba's* movements are based on feel rather than formalised steps; as a consequence, it is rarely danced competitively and, when done so, the **winners** are generally deemed to be the first couple to *arribar a casa* ('get to home base').

Naturally, none of this could take place without music, and San Sombrèro has no shortage of *tumbe*, or **traditional dance ensembles**, to provide the pulsating rhythms required.

A typical *tumbe* band (below) consists of six people, five musicians and one in charge of bringing the **checked** shirts. Featuring **complex percussion** and vocal parts, you're likely to hear everything, from the bass-like thud of conga drums and shaking of maracas, to the tapping together of hardwood clave sticks and **high-pitched yelp** of the person who just hit his finger with one.

Seeing and hearing an authentic *tumbe* **band** play live is an experience you are not likely to forget. Most *tumbe* songs follow a set pattern. First, a long lyrical vocal **melody** unfolds, allowing the lead singer an opportunity to express **emotions** and mention anyone who might have left their lights on in the car park. Then, on a cue from the band leader, the **rhythm** tightens up, the chorus commences and the bass player stops drinking so he can actually join in. From here, things get pretty **frenetic** as everyone begins to improvise, often in several different **keys**. The lead singer will offer several *inspiraciones*, or **emotional** thoughts, although overt political statements or gripes about his percentage of the door takings are not unheard of.

Popular Music

Rock 'n' roll is fast growing in popularity and everywhere you'll see **long-haired youths** – *roqueros* – wearing Metallica **T-shirts**. These kids tend to be fans of heavy metal with a Latin feel, known as *Slambarda*. Rock 'n' roll's popularity has only been limited by the **irregularity** of electricity supplies. Fans are, however, notoriously patient and if a guitarist is in the middle of a screeching solo when the **power** goes off they will simply wait, often for several hours, while **roadies** hunt for the requisite number of car batteries.

LOS POPOLOS

One of San Sombrèro's most enduring and well-known musical duos, Los Popolos, was formed in 1974 by brothers Pepi and Luis Valleta. Dedicated to traditional folk music, Los Popolos use a plethora of instruments including guitars, claves, guiro and, indeed, a plethora. Their music has often been described as 'timeless', a reference to their frequent inability to maintain a beat. Over the decades Los Popolos have played for no fewer than 12 different presidents and their rousing anthem 'Atumba! Tre!' became the unofficial theme song for General Faruz Gustamo's 1997 military coup. At their farewell concert in May 2005 Los Popolos were rewarded with three standing ovations, one of them voluntary.

Marracos bands such as this are often employed to stand outside a shop, not only entertaining passers-by, but also helping to advertise the clothing range available inside.

Country and western music is also represented by stars such as Manuel 'Hillbilli' Hortez [above] who has taken the roots of traditional San Sombrèran folk music and added a large hat.

SIZZLIN' SILVIO!

Considered one of the greatest Latin American recording artists in the world today, Silvio Enrique got his first taste of performing as a young boy in the school choir where his sensuous dancing and gyrating hips soon drew him to the attention of the parish priest (who was later charged and jailed).

As a child Silvio appeared in a few TV commercials (mainly for cigarettes) before landing a spot with San Sombrèro's most popular Latin boy band, Fagoto. Despite being the youngest member (their average age was, in fact, 43) Silvio soon proved himself immensely talented and the next five years were spent maintaining a gruelling regime of touring, recording and hair-care.

In 1996 Espero fans were shocked to learn that Silvio had left the group. The group was even more stunned, as he'd taken their truck. Silvio spent the next year in New York trying to make it as a solo performer but times were tough. He decided to give acting a go but, lacking any experience, there was only one option – Mexican TV. It was here he landed the role of Dr Jose Jose, in the long-running daytime soap opera *Adobe Mi Amora*.

But music remained Silvio's first love and it wasn't long before he was back in the studio recording his first solo album. As fate would have it, this album was almost never released after it was discovered that its title *Los Mucho Puerto Exitos Callabraca Mos Nueveo* wouldn't fit on the CD cover. But the album did eventually come out (unlike Silvio, who continues a close relationship with his 'personal stylist') and went on to sell three million copies. Admittedly, this was largely Silvio's own family back in San Sombrèro, but news of his success soon spread.

His next album, *Loving Me is a Pleasure* was over three years in the making (although nine months of that time was spent re-touching his hair on the cover photo) and went on to receive a Latin Grammy for 'Best Pop Performance Without a Shirt'. In 2002 Silvio released his first English-language album, a move that surprised many San Sombrèran fans who hadn't realised their hero spoke English. But, as Silvio himself proudly declared, 'For me English is of language the communicationing, and for that I make no apalogoly'. Over the past decade Silvio has scored a string of Top Ten hits, with Latin classics such as 'Be Careful With My Heart', 'Show Me Your Love', 'Let Me Love You for a Night', 'Let Me Love You for Half an Hour' and the infectious 'You Drive Me Crazy'.*

Due to a poor translation, the English version of this song was released as 'You Crazy Driver' and actually featured in a British road safety TV campaign.

Literature

San Sombrèrans love books. Literary and **poetry readings** are regularly held throughout the country and are always well attended, especially the so-called 'Rum Recitals' during which the **librarian** reads poetry and the guests drink.

Many of San Sombrèro's finest 20th century authors such as Paulo Guira (1902–88) and Felix Loynaz (1904–67) were forced to flee the country because of their strong **anti-government** stance. Others, such as **controversial essayist** Gabriel Lima (1912–75) were also exiled, although in his case it was more to do with the fact that he'd been caught **robbing** a bank.

CORTENO

A man. An accordian. And a ballad tradition dating back centuries. That's the magic of the corteno, a style of folk song renowned for the length and detail of its lyrics. A typical corteno will often take over an hour just to reach the first chorus.

Typical lyrics read as follows:

'I'm going to sing a corteno
About a man I know
He is a man who is
known by me
And his name is
Vasquez Abajeno.

He comes from
Los Vias de Muejra
Down by Sinpaco Way
Near where the
Chicopa River
Runs past the bridge
of Del Marle
Just back from the highway
Turn left at the Plaza Core
Two doors up from
the old oak tree

The house with
the white fence
Not the wooden hut
with the cactus
That belongs to his sister
It's diagonally opposite
With a new verandah out
the front.

Let me draw you a map…'

CARLA BONEZ (1961–93) was one of San Sombrèro's most tortured, yet brilliant modern poets. Eventually the demands of caring for her family and writing became too much and she took her own life, leaving behind a poignant suicide note: 'Dinner is in the oven. So am I.'

San Sombrèrans are keen readers, mainly of comics and erotic fiction.

Just another day at work for this San Sombrèran street sweeper.

Art

The history of San Sombrèran **painting** can be divided into three basic stages. The first began in 1817 with the **foundation** of the Academia Nacional, a school strongly influenced by Neo-Classicism. The second developed over a century later when *Nuevo Modernismo*, a movement influenced by the European **avant-garde** created a universally **comprehensible** idiom that expressed the essence of San Sombrèran identity. The third was **cigarette** billboards.

Modern San Sombrèran painting brims with **colour and vitality**. With daubs of paint, fleeting light and wild colour, many of these works are considered best viewed from a **distance**. Such as Brazil.

FASCINATING FACT

While Spanish colonial artists only ever depicted nudes in a discretely modest manner typical of the time, there was no such prurience from local painters. So celebrated was the human form that, in many San Sombrèran landscapes, you'll note the fig leaves are covered over with penises.

Since 1980, professional house painters in San Sombrèro have been banned from working under the influence of hallucinogenic drugs.

Many San Sombrèran Arts Festivals culminate with a rueda, in which any painters, writers, actors or directors who have been critical of the government are 'honoured' by being ceremoniously dangled upside down from a rope.

Theatre

San Sombrèro has a small, but active theatre **scene**, with half a dozen dramatic societies across the country. The main focus tends to be **slapstick comedies** set to **trumpet** music, a style that influences just about all productions (a recent performance of *Henry V* had the **eponymous monarch** stumble on stage in clown's pants, only to then be hit by cream pies). Highly politicised pro-government theatre also features heavily and most citizens are required as part of **national service** to see at least one performance of *El Presidente Benevolento* – a lengthy **operatic discourse** on the wisdom and popularity of San Sombrèro's head of state.

Film

San Sombrèrans are **passionate movie-goers**, possibly because cinemas are often the only air-conditioned **buildings** in town. But the country does have a healthy **home-grown film industry**. One of its earliest cinematographers was Tomas Calles (1934–96) who, despite any formal training, produced over 30 feature films, some in **colour** and quite a few in focus.

The San Sombrèran **government** closely controls cinema and this has, understandably, stymied much **creative expression**. Official government policy favours films of a 'socially-redeeming' nature, mainly historical dramas, Biblical **epics** and soft porn.

San Sombrèran films are traditionally recorded in Spanish, then dubbed into Italian before being re-dubbed into English and, finally, re-re-dubbed back into Spanish. (Interestingly, they are then screened with Spanish sub-titles)

THE WILD WEST
San Sombrèro has long been famous for its 'spaghetti westerns', most of which were shot in the west of the country. During the 1970's boom, so many sets were built for these films that they actually became real towns, boasting a unique architectural style known as façadio – a plywood front held up by trusses.

LIGHTS, ACTION, CAMERA
The most respected of San Sombrèro's contemporary filmmakers would have to be Manu Hostales whose style could best be described a 'magical realism', in that – no matter what the context – his female character's clothes will magically fall from their body. Hostales' most successful film was *Charangos Dos* (1994), a **stark drama** set inside a girls' school, that broke box office records as well as several United Nations covenants on the protection of child actors.

CORAJOSO!   **COMBA**

RAMON FUSILLEZ es...

EL PAUN

RAMON FUSILLEZ • BONIFACIO (BOBO) JUMINEZ • FILOMENA (FIFI) TUB(
CON **CUTENIO (CUCU) FILLIOL** • GUION ESTEBAN PURELLEZ • DIRECTOR HERNAN C
DE LA NOVELA "EL MONSIGNOR FLATULENTO" DE CAMILLO (CACA) NUNEZ

EN COLOR!   VISION-PAN

Without doubt San Sombrèro's most popular and enduring movie star, Ramon Fusillez burst onto the silver screen with the classic Western tale of *El Pauncho*. The plot was simple: by day, he's an ill-tempered, hard-drinking, overweight parish priest. By night, he's much the same, but with a mask, allowing the mysterious renegade to roam the country at will, stealing from the rich and lending to the poor. *El Pauncho* was released in 1967 and, over the coming decades, was followed by a string of sequels, including:

El Pauncho Rides Again, *The Curse of El Pauncho*, *The Legend of El Pauncho*, *El Pauncho at Large*, *Carry On El Pauncho*, *El Pauncho and the Harlem Globetrotters Visit the Moon* and the final, somewhat ill-fated *El Pauncho Lives!* (a film shot several month's after the lead actor's death and consisting largely of long-shots depicting a poorly matched body double falling off a horse).

TV

San Sombrèran TV involves a fairly standard mix of news, sport, sitcoms and shows involving **bathroom renovations**. But without doubt the most popular programmes – as in a lot of Latin America – are the *telenovelas*. These long-running soap operas are so popular that at certain times of the day the **streets** can almost seem empty as eager viewers gather round their TVs to view the latest instalment. (It's said that notorious rebel leader Victor Demirra was only ever captured because government troops managed to sneak up on him during the **wedding** episode of his favourite show.) So pervasive is the *telenovela* style, that even San Sombrèro's nightly news is presented by a **handsome man** who stares moodily into the camera as it zooms in at the end of each story. The bulletin often concludes with the **weathergirl** slapping him. However, the plot of most *telenovelas* is not always easy to pick up, especially for short-term **visitors**. Here is a brief guide provided by the **producers**) to some of San Sombrèro's most popular long-running series…

Barrio D'Amor (NEIGHBOURHOOD OF LOVE)
Isabella lives in Cucaracha City with her overweight, overbearing and over-acting stepfather. When she was only 12 years old, her real father abandoned her and her mother fell into a deep depression and died two episodes later. Isabella's stepfather has recently lost all his money, along with his memory, in a stock market crash. Through sheer effort and determination, Isabella managed to graduate from medical school, but she clings to her dream of one day becoming a dancer. Isabella also helps out her boyfriend Marcelo, who is studying to be more handsome.

Dias D'Amor (DAYS OF LOVE)
The story started 10 years ago, when six sisters and their stepfather had an automobile accident. Before the car exploded, the oldest sister, Luisa, managed to rescue only Marissa, with the rest of the family presumed dead, but that turns out not to be true. After the crash, she receives a knock on the head. When she wakes up, she has lost her memory – meaning she can't remember she has amnesia from a previous car accident. Meanwhile Marissa meets Cesar, a man who will disappoint her, and Carlos, a young man from the lower middle-class who pleasures her until he meets Cesar and finds another way to disappoint her.

Oceano D'Amor (OCEAN OF LOVE)

After an accident leaves them both orphans with amnesia, sisters Alma and Aida move in with their evil aunt who wants to take away their inheritance. Aida meets Antonio who by day works as a boxer and by night as an ecologist, fighting against the deforestation.* Angry at the relationship, the evil aunt starts a fire and Aida is horribly disfigured, so badly that she is forced to wear a mask. But love proves stronger than disfigurement and Claudia proposes to Aida, on condition she keeps the mask on, except in the dark. *As Oceano D'Amor was sponsored by one of San Sombrèro's largest logging companies, this character was written out – via a nasty death – after just a few episodes.

Amor D'Amor (LOVE OF LOVE)

Blanca is a beautiful young woman, with a great desire to live, despite having heart disease. She works as a fashion designer, and makes a wedding dress for Raquela who is going to marry Jose Manuel. But just before the wedding Jose Manuel finally realises who it is he really loves. Blanca's younger brother. Before he can declare this love, Raquela dies in an accident and at the same time Blanca has a heart attack. In order to save Blanca, they transplant Raquela's heart into her and also perform comprehensive cosmetic surgery, causing Jose Manuel to give up his dream of being a veterinarian and fall in love with her. *(Amor D'Amor is considered a breakthrough programme for San Sombrèro as it was the first TV series where no-one gets amnesia. Unfortunately, the scriptwriters did, and all of Series Two was repeated after Series Five. Remarkably, no-one noticed.)*

DOG MAN

Without doubt, one of the most popular men on San Sombrèran TV would have to be Pedro Lopezco, star of the long-running series **Animal Logic.** *(By day he's a blind vet. By night he solves cold cases involving pets with the assistance of his guide dog, 20/20.)*

Sport

The San Sombrèran Government's encouragement of physical activity began in 1954 when they moved to phase out **cigar smoking** during school hours. Since then a range of state-sponsored **health** and fitness programmes have ensured San Sombrèro's success on the world **sporting** stage. Strong, talented students are often singled out for special training and most cities boast a *Centro Deportivo* (Sports Centre) with **tennis courts**, gymnasium, pool and pharmaceutical laboratories.

DID YOU KNOW?
At the 1996 Atlanta Olympics San Sombrèro boasted the only team to enter the opening ceremony on board a carnival float.

Leading figures in sport include boxer Luis Gonzalez (see opposite), baseballer Javier Estez and Olympic **star** Ricarda Suarez who, in 1995, broke the world **high jump record**, only to be disqualified after it was revealed he was being shot at by border guards when he made his **epic leap**. San Sombrèro has also produced some excellent long-distance swimmers, most of whom have made it to **Miami** and are refusing to return home.

Soccer (*Futbol*) is hugely popular in San Sombrèro and every **weekend** there are matches being played. As in many Latin American countries, most **stadiums** have moats, fences and barbed wire to keep **rival fans** apart. But, due to endemic violence, in San Sombrèro competing **teams** are also separated, with the ground itself divided in two by an electric fence. Sadly, this has not stopped numerous ugly altercations and most **referees** now have the choice of issuing a yellow card, red card or a dose of capsicum spray.

Corey Writes... For the Adventure Traveller
No need to be a spectator man, San Sombrèro offers a heap of adventure sport options. On top of the usual mountain-biking, canoeing, fishing, climbing, white-water rafting, sea kayaking, dog sledding, tandem hang-gliding and kite surfing there's also a new version of shark cage diving in which both you and the shark are placed in an underwater cage and left to fend for yourselves. Awesome!

LUIS GONZALEZ – BORN TO BOX

One of San Sombrèro's most famous sportsmen, Luis Gonzalez was **a dazzling athlete** who enthralled the public with his ability to knock out opponents, promoters, spectators, critics and – on one memorable occasion – even himself.

Born in San Abandonio in 1932, Luis bordered on being a bit stocky, with short muscular arms and legs. However, he possessed **unusual physical strength** thanks to his father, whom he had to carry home most nights from the pub, and – by the age of just eight – he could bench press a donkey.

His first experience of boxing came via his aunts, Elva and Raquel, who lived nearby and would often **exchange punches**. Academically, however, Luis struggled and in the summer of 1941, he announced that he would not be returning to school. In some ways this was a sensible decision, as he'd burnt the place to the ground a few days before, but his mother and father were not happy with their son's intention to take up boxing full time. However, Luis was determined and his parents – realising he had made up his mind (and weighed 48 more **pounds** than both of them combined) – agreed to let him become a professional boxer.

Luis immediately started on a strict training regimen, involving miles of roadwork, gym and weights. At night he was sent into neighbouring bars to pick a **fight** with whoever was drinking there. Luis would also work out at the beach, where his coach would have him tread water for as long as possible while throwing **underwater punches**. Not only did this give Luis enormous body strength, it also allowed him to become the first man in history to knock out a dolphin.

From his debut fight in 1942 (won on points) to his comeback triumph at the age of 73 (won on a walking frame), Luis' career reads like a Hollywood movie. Within just a few years he had taken out the world heavyweight championship, married a model and released his own range of **fat-free cooking** appliances. A personal high came in 1950 when he fought at the 1950 Olympics (despite having been selected as a shot-putter). Luis Gonzalez defended his title six times and holds the distinction of being the world's first **heavyweight champion** to retire without a felony conviction.

Beisbol

Another of San Sombrèro's most-popular sports. On any given day one can see kids playing **baseball** in the street, dreaming of making it to the 'big league'. And some have indeed done so, none more **famous** than Cucarachan born Quinto Emirez who, in 1971, led his team to

a **National Championship**. A year later he led them to Florida, in an unsuccessful attempt to **defect en masse**. After many more years at the top, Emirez retired from baseball in 1976 to embark on a short-lived TV career, his tonight show *Here's Quinto* being axed early in its run. Emirez then worked for a short period as a **sporting journalist** before returning to his first loves – cocaine and prostitutes.

BARRO

An athlete warms up as he prepares for *barro*, a reverse form of the high jump that requires participants to limbo under the bar. The national record now stands at a miniscule 9.23cm.

In many parts of San Sombrèro soccer is confined to the dry season.

Bullfighting

While soccer and baseball remain popular, there is nothing more quintessentially San Sombrèran than bullfighting. This sport has a huge following, especially in rural areas where not only the bull but also the **bullfighter** is routinely killed. San Sombrèran *toreros* are considered amongst the world's most reckless and the crowd will **whoop and cheer** with each injury sustained. The intervention of animal rights activists has only increased their enjoyment, with **spectators** loving nothing more than the sight of a placard-waving **protestor** trying to fend off 800kg of rampaging beef.

During the first act the trumpets sound and the *toreros* will tire the bull out. The second act sees the bull stabbed with multiple **metal spikes**, each delivered to the blast of a trumpet. In the third act a **sword** is driven between the charging animal's **shoulder blades**, accompanied by ever-louder trumpet blasts. The fourth act involves hog-tying the trumpeter.

San Sombrèran toreros are frequently frustrated by the fact that local bulls are incredibly docile and often require severe provocation in order to get them to fight.

San Sombrèro v Brazil (El Classico de '63)

For many, the classic showdown between arch-rivals San Sombrèro and Brazil on 5 June 1963 will forever be remembered as one of the greatest football matches ever played. For those fans lucky enough to have been there, every minute of this International Unfriendly remains forever etched in the memory.

After the usual pre-match preliminaries of meeting the president, singing the national anthem and ceremoniously sacrificing the team mascot, play got underway.

- In the 5th minute, the Brazilian centre-forward was carried off on a stretcher after being struck on the back of the head by an object thrown from a small group of fanatical San Sombrèrans. The culprit was apprehended and escorted back to his position in midfield. The referee then rushed in and immediately showed a yellow card to the policeman.
- Just before half-time, the game had to be stopped because of a pitch-invasion. It took over 15 minutes for the goat-herder to remove his flock.
- During the half-time interval all players were summoned back onto the field to officially meet San Sombrèro's new president, his predecessor having been overthrown half an hour earlier in a surprise military coup.
- In a frenetic start to the second half, San Sombrèran striker Raul Jimenez struck the frame of the goal an amazing three times in 30 seconds. The fact he did so with the head of the Brazilian goalkeeper earned him a red card. The referee was immediately sent off.
- In the 63rd minute, Bombumba Fartez (the 'Flying Elephant') was substituted after a severe attack of gout. He was replaced by the extremely quick Pepe 'Speedy' Gonzalez, who immediately went into action, charging half the length of the ground while weaving his way past flat-footed defenders. His now-legendary run was eventually stopped when the referee informed him the ball was still in his goalkeeper's hands.

At full-time the scores were tied, leaving only one option – a penalty shoot-out. The ensuing gun battle lasted for an hour, after which surviving members of both teams exchanged jumpers and hostages.

THE TEAM

JOSE LULA

JOAQUINTO PEPERUNYAS

LUALDO MAROCCAS

PEDRITO BOM

MILTON BANNANNA

CUCUCHO RUALDINHO

PABLO ZIETTA

GIGI SPALYETA

RAUL JIMENEZ

BOMBUMBA FARTEZ

JUAN CARLOS REBEBUMBA

MANAGER: F. TALBACO

(absent, whereabouts unknown)

SMOKERS' PARADISE

Smoking remains a major problem in San Sombrèro, despite various government education programs. Large tobacco companies exert such influence that a recent attempt to place health warnings on cigarette packets resulted in the following:

'Warning – the link between smoking and ill health is yet to be conclusively proved.'

'Smoking. Come on – you know it makes you look cool.'

'Jesus Smoked.'

A new health advisory message, suggesting tobacco use leads to increased genital size, is due for release later this year.

The Economy

San Sombrèro is remarkably free from the **poverty** that afflicts much of Central America. Most of its people own a home, or some form of upright structure, and even its **shantytowns** are architect-designed.

Of course, there are problems and chronic **shortages** do exist, such as **pharmaceuticals**, automotive parts and electronic goods. Toilet seats are still officially classified as a 'luxury item'.

It has often been said that San Sombrèro's greatest asset is its **people**, although tobacco would clearly run a close second. That said, one the greatest challenges facing industry is that its people lack a definable **work ethic**. The long-term unemployed are envied for their **lifestyle** and no amount of coaxing from factory owners or bosses can lift productivity. Some have resorted to booking **motivational speakers** but, more often than not, even these people can't be bothered showing up.

San Sombrèro - Top Six Exports

1. Coffee

2. Sequins

3. Sloths

4. Hammocks

5. Electric fans

6. Miss World Runners-Up

Tobacco

San Sombrèran tobacco is justifiably regarded as amongst the **best** in the world. About 40,000 metric tons are produced per annum, enough for every **smoker** to enjoy five cigars a day for as long as they live (about 32 years).

Sugar

San Sombrèro is also one of the world's **major sugar growers**. For many years so much was produced that, to avoid an oversupply, the **surplus** was 'exported' (shipped out to sea and dumped overboard), which could explain the high incidence of **tooth decay** amongst local **sharks**. To reduce this excess production, sugar is added to just about everything, even salt.

Coffee

When settlers planted the first coffee beans back in 1577, few could have foreseen the **impact** this crop would come to have. Within a century, coffee had transformed San Sombrèro from a **sleepy colonial backwater** to one that was very much awake. San Sombrèran coffee beans contain the highest concentration of caffeine in the world and are **keenly sought** by long distance truck drivers all over Central America.

Beef

San Sombrèran cattle are amongst the most **obese** in the world, as many suffer from a condition known as *Lazy Cow Disease*. As a result, **local beef** is extremely **marbled** and so high in fat content that during emergencies select cuts of meat can be burnt as candles.

Tourism

Tourism is not new to San Sombrèro. **Holidaymakers** first started coming to the country during the early 19th century and, in 1833, the **eastern province** of Lambarda became the first place in the world to introduce a departure tax.

SMOKING STAR
San Sombrèro proudly ranks as one of the world's largest producers of cigars and smoking-related products. US tobacconist Luis Vellasquez , inventor of the *cigarello,* was born in Cucaracha City and no visit is complete without a trip to view his body lying in state there, inside its own specially designed humidor.

FAST FACT
A major breakthrough took place in the 1990s when the San Sombrèran Institute for Caffeine Research successfully produced the first instant coffee bean.

Ecology & Environment

Despite its best efforts, San Sombrèro has struggled to preserve much of its precious **natural environment**. Widespread logging and mining operations have decimated large tracts of rainforest, while **illegal poaching** has reached such a point that over 70% of native bird life now lives in cages inside hotel lobbies. But the government has been active in promoting **sustainable development** via alternative energy projects. In addition to solar and wind power, they are currently funding an ambitious scheme to harness power from electric eels that could, if **successful**, see the entire Rio Pongo Valley **fish-fuelled** within a decade.

As well as its jungles and forests, San Sombrèro's **marine areas** are also in need of greater protection. Cucaracha Harbour is indisputably one of the most **polluted** bodies of water in the world, and sections of the mighty Aruzul River downstream from Vernharo are so heavily **contaminated** that a recent *E. coli* test of its water failed to find any actual water.

Illegal trade in animals remains a major problem for San Sombrèro, where a black market jaguar **pelt** can easily fetch $US4000. With such high **prices** it comes as no surprise that several of the country's **big cats** have even been known to sell their own skin.

Helena Writes... For the Eco-Traveller
Wherever one travels you have an impact on the environment, and it is the responsible traveller's duty to make sure this impact is a positive one and that you are not contributing to the corruption or degradation of the place visited. Some of the most rewarding trips I've made are when I've decided not to go.

The Effluentez Cascadas just below the township of Turdos, where scientists estimate almost half a million litres of raw effluent flows every day.

San Sombrèro's rare rotondo *waterlily grows in three sizes: small, medium and family.*

Flora

Despite four centuries of devastating **deforestation**, extensive tracts of San Sombrèro remain cloaked in **green**. Admittedly, much of these are soccer fields, but significant regions of **pristine vegetation** remain.

San Sombrèro boasts 6270 higher-plant **species**, of which nearly 30% are endemic and 65% **prickly**. Indigenous tree species include cedar, cypress, pine, rosewood and the **noxious willow**. Cactus is also harvested, not for its wood, but its spikes, which are turned into 'toothpricks'.

In terms of vegetation, San Sombrèro's main areas are, in order:
1. *Lowland rainforest*
2. *Previously logged deforested rainforest*
3. *Re-deforested forest*
4. *Cactus*
5. *Urban Sprawl*
6. *Quarries*

*San Sombrèro boasts more than 2000 separate species of cactus. Indeed, its **floral emblem** is the fluted cactus, or **cactos dildos** (above). In recent years scientists have begun experimenting with hybrid breeds of **edible cacti**, and are currently working on such varieties as the cactusberry, cactapple and cacteloupe.*

San Sombrèro has many species of coconut palm. In fact, during June–July, the odds of being struck by a falling coconut are so high that safety helmets are compulsory in all coastal regions.

Fauna

While the fauna of San Sombrèro is nowhere as rich as when the Spaniards first arrived, many **species** still survive. The best way to see these animals is to join an organised wildlife watching tour, although care should be exercised in choosing these, especially any organisations offering 'accommodation, food, transport and ammo'.

San Sombrèro boast 23 species of venomous **snake**, however, visitors should not be overly alarmed as these timid creatures will rarely attack humans unless they are cornered, protecting a nest, or bored.

The country is also home to one of the world's rarest **frogs** (*Sminthillus limbatus*), a creature so tiny it takes almost 100 to make a bowl of soup.

The three-toed **sloth** spends much of its time hanging upside down from trees, sleeping up to 18 hours a day and descending to the ground to excrete just once a week. Surprisingly, they're highly intelligent and, in 1998, several came close to being elected to local parliament.

There are numerous species of **monkey** found in San Sombrèro. The most common are noisy **howler monkeys** whose roar carries over many kilometres, as does their smell.

One of the larger predators found in San Sombrèro's rainforests is the **cougar**

(*Felis Concolor*). It takes skill and luck to spot these wildcats – unless, of course, one starts gnawing on your foot – in which case their presence is fairly obvious.

Whilst rare, the diminutive **jaguar** also makes its home in the county's inland forests. One of the smallest 'big cats' in the world, these creatures only grow to a length of about five feet, including the tail, which often makes up four of these.

The magnificent **puma** still inhabits many areas. As well as feeding on deer, these sleek creatures have been known to attack domestic animals such as sheep and tour groups.

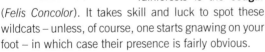

The carnivorous San Sombrèran **tapir** (*Tapirus terrestris*) has sharp teeth and survives by hunting other mammals. About the size of a stocky pony, it is, in fact, related to the horse, and several years ago an attempt was made to train and race these animals, a venture quickly abandoned after one of the minor place-getters ate its own jockey.

Leaf-cutter **ants** inhabit most lowland areas and can often be seen in columns carrying bits of food or leaves twice their size. One of these ants was once spotted making its way back to the nest with a set of stolen golf clubs but this report has never been independently verified.

The marsh **deer** is a small, reddish animal that can easily be recognised for its oversized antlers, some of which grow up to 80cm in length. They are generally found in forested regions, tangled up in ivy or thick shrub.

Watch out for the Caribbean **hairy tarantula**, found throughout the country. This fearsome looking spider is so hirsute it has dreadlocks.

San Sombrèro is a major stopover for migratory **water-fowl**, including the flightless **kelp goose**, a bird whose annual migration involves an epic 120km waddle.

The San Sombrèran dolphin is described as being similar to a Bottlenose Dolphin *except for having **shorter dorsal fins** and a slightly saltier taste.*

The world wildlife trade is a global industry, threatening many of this planet's most vulnerable species. Visit our website to find details on how you can help fight the scourge of illegal animal smuggling. For those less concerned, this same site also contains a list of outlets where eager shoppers can pick up stuffed animals, fur coats and feathered headwear.

Shopping

San Sombrèro is a great place to pick up a **bargain**, provided you know what you're looking for. Amongst the best buys are hand-carved wooden artefacts such as **statues** and **bowls**.

Hand-carved **electronic goods** are also available but less highly recommended. Be advised that objects bearing a **sticker** *hecho en San Sombrèro* ('made in San Sombrèro') have often been manufactured in other countries – it is only the sticker itself that was made locally.

San Sombrèran **pottery** is not generally of great quality and most ceramic items have a tendency to **leak**, crack, split, crumble or – in some reported cases – explode due to tiny **pockets of air** which are trapped during the firing process.

This aside, they are cheap and make a good **gift** for someone you are unlikely to see again. San Sombrèran **leather** is cheap but not particularly supple; in fact, it's so stiff some was recently tested by **NASA** as a possible material for heat shield tiles on the space shuttle.

SMOOTH SMOKE!

San Sombrèran cigars are considered inferior to those of Cuba, often being machine-made and held together with tape or fuse wire. If you are planning to buy local cigars, insist on *Coabaina* brand; these are hand-made and, according to the manufacturers, rolled on the buttocks of a virgin.

HAGGLING

When haggling in San Sombrèro, the usual tricks apply: never show the least sign of enthusiasm, and walking away will almost always guarantee a price cut. (The same rules apply when dating in San Sombrèro.)

*Outdoor tourist **markets** are held regularly throughout San Sombrèro and are a great place to pick up arts and crafts. Most of these markets have a policy stating that stallholders can only sell goods they have grown, made or stolen themselves.*

Helena Writes... For the Eco-Traveller
Many goods, such as antiques or native art, are not allowed by law to be taken out of the country. With other products, such as folk instruments, the government offers a cash incentive to encourage their removal. Remember, exporting anything made with macaw feathers is prohibited unless it is a macaw, in which case removing the plumage is considered illegal.

Shopper's Tip

Many San Sombrèran craftsmen specialise in items that may be difficult, if not impossible, to bring back into your country, due to **customs regulations**. Amongst these so-called '**hazardous**' goods are blowpipes, flick knives, push knives, pistol grip crossbows, nunchakas, knuckle dusters, electronic fly swatters and some local rum. Luckily, many handicraft stores offer a discrete prohibited goods **wrapping service**; for just a few dollars your purchase can be **concealed** inside a teddy bear, musical instrument, or religious statue. There's also a **premium service** in which a shop assistant will swallow the item and travel home with you.

Traveller's Tip 👍

One of the most common items for sale at San Sombrèran markets are *cineceros* (ashtrays) made of stuffed frogs or snake skin. Visitors are advised not to buy these as doing so contributes to the destruction of the country's endemic wildlife. They also tend to catch fire.

A lack of stock rarely prevents San Sombrèran fashion stores from promoting their new season's range with a window display featuring nude mannequins bearing the phrase 'watch this space'.

Health & Safety

No **vaccinations** or inoculations are necessary to visit San Sombrèro as government programmes have eliminated most attention-grabbing **nasties** such as small pox and yellow fever many years ago. That said, travellers should be aware of the risks associated with poor **hygiene**, untreated water, mosquito bites, undressed open cuts and unprotected sex, especially when they are all a result of the one date.

Many problems arise from a basic lack of **sanitation**. Avoid food that looks like it has been on display for a while and remember that the phrase 'Best Before June 2020' is an overly optimistic **guarantee** not based on any scientific data.

San Sombrèro has a reasonably good system of **hospitals** and clinics so you should have little trouble finding prompt **medical care**. However, be warned, most hospitals in the country are staffed by **trainee doctors** eager to gain 'hands-on' experience.

All international **hotels** have a '24-hour nurse' (so named because this is often the number of hours she or he has spent **training**). These para-medicos will visit your room and treat **minor ailments** as well as – for a small tip – re-stock your mini-bar. (Don't forget to tip 10%.)

Tina Writes...
For the Cautious Traveller
Before leaving home it's a good idea to make photocopies of your passport, credit cards and insurance details in case these are lost or stolen while you are away. Then make copies of these copies, along with a detailed will, which should be stored in a waterproof vault. Then cancel your trip.

Traveller's Tip
While no inoculations are required for San Sombrèro, it's worth visiting your doctor a few weeks before leaving to have him x-ray your kidneys and liver. This could prove valuable if you have organs stolen and need to make an insurance claim.

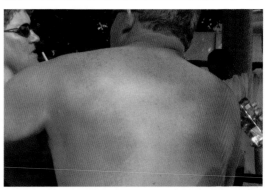

Over exposure to the sun is a real problem in San Sombrèro. Your safest bet is to get a spray-on tan or, for British tourists, a spray-on burn.

Drugs – Legal

Pharmacies are notoriously under-stocked and visitors requiring **medication** are better advised to seek out a local drug dealer. Not only are prices cheaper, many of them offer detailed **advice**. If you do visit a *farmacia*, be warned that many still stock drugs such as Expro-Viaform and Texacone, which cause **optic nerve damage** and have been banned elsewhere. Do not be fooled by the pharmacist's assurances or any buy-ten-get-one-free medication offers.

San Sombrèro also produces a wide range of medicines made from natural ingredients, including **syrups**, tinctures and vegetable essences. These are freely available and **cost** next to nothing. The fact they do next to nothing should be viewed as only a minor drawback.

Malaria is a problem only in isolated areas. If you plan on spending much time in the mountains or **rainforests** of San Sombrèro it's worth taking a course of chloroquine, starting one week before you arrive and continuing for the rest of your natural life.

Rabies is prevalent throughout San Sombrèro, especially amongst the many **dogs** and **monkeys** that roam its streets. Your best protection is a series of **shots** – preferably aimed at the animal's head.

Drugs – Illegal

While drugs such as marijuana are technically illegal in San Sombrèro, **officials** will look the other way provided you possess only small amounts; less than 5kg is generally presumed to be for **personal use**. Less clear are the large number of naturally occurring drugs used widely in San Sombrèro – there are more species of **psychoactive plants** found here than any other country in the world. Many of these, such as hallucinogenic mushrooms, are tolerated only if used as part of **religious rituals** or nightclub visits.

Helena Writes... For the Eco-Traveller
Mosquito repellents and coils contain harmful chemicals that can damage the local ecosystem. A far friendlier and less damaging method of deterring these insects is to simply urinate on yourself. This keeps away mozzies, sandflies, ticks and, in most cases, other people.

Safety

It doesn't take long before visitors to San Sombrèro encounter some form of petty **crime**. Even on some flights in, **petty theft** is so rife that passengers are warned not to lose sight of their sick-bags. Simple **common sense** tends to be the best protection.

- Be very suspicious about taking a ride in a cab where a 'friend' is **accompanying** the driver. San Sombrèran taxi drivers don't have friends.
- Minimise the risk of mugging by simply avoiding deserted areas such as **pedestrian underpasses** or **cultural** centres.
- If driving always park in designated parking lots or, when that's not possible, accept the offer of **local** men or boys to watch over your **car** while you're gone. They will not always be able to prevent theft but, for a few **dollars**, will provide a detailed description of who stole your vehicle.

Traffic is probably your greatest danger. Remember, when crossing the street in San Sombrèro, **pedestrians** do not have any right of way. If possible, look for a marked **pedestrian crossing**; cars will not stop but, if hit, the ambulance will have less trouble finding you.

The truth is, **violent crime** remains pleasantly absent from **the streets** of San Sombrèro. In fact, studies have shown 79% of physical **assaults** take place within parliament.

In up-market restaurants and nightclubs many restrooms have an attendant who is responsible for dispensing toilet paper. In many cases this will be made from bark and should only be used with caution.

San Sombrèro leads the world in mystifying safety signs. The first warns against the dangers of dancing on uneven surfaces, the second cautions against crossing the road on a full stomach.

In an Emergency

San Sombrèro's **police** are generally honest but, remember, they are also badly paid. Many are convicted **criminals** who have simply accepted a job in the police force as an alternative to **prison**. Graft is common and most visitors – especially motorists – will find themselves accused of some **violation**. In this instance the subject of a 'fine' will generally be raised. These small **bribes** are known as *mordidas* 'bites' and are an accepted way of doing business with any uniformed official, be they a **police officer**, border guard or parish priest.

The San Sombrèran **legal system** is based on the Central American Civil Code, which assumes both your guilt and the judge's **dishonesty**, unless proved otherwise. If jailed, you should be offered one **phone call**; whilst it can be to your consulate, a more useful option would be to ring a **pizza delivery service** as you are unlikely to see any food for quite a few days. Under San Sombrèran law, you can be held up for up to 72 hours on **suspicion**, after which time you must either be charged or taken down from the wall.

FASCINATING FACT
Under the San Sombrèran legal code, judges may use their gavels to either call for order or to strike the accused.

Petty theft is so rife in many San Sombrèran cities that coined-operated public phone booths must be protected by armed guards.

SENIORS
Older travellers are warmly welcomed in San Sombrèro, especially by pickpockets, who tend to find them an easy target.

THE PROPINA
The *Propina*, or tip, is an endemic part of doing business in San Sombrèro. Whilst not essential, it's remarkable how a few banknotes complete paperwork that would otherwise take weeks, find a seat on a previously full bus or lead to the lifting of environmental restrictions for a proposed coastal resort development.

Women Travellers

San Sombrèro is a typically 'macho' Latin American nation, and **single women** can expect their fair share of **catcalls**, whistles or propositions. If you feel someone has over-stepped the mark, notify a police officer, unless of course it was the police officer making the **improper advances**, in which case just keep walking. To prevent hassles, avoid wearing skimpy shorts, short skirts, or **sleeveless tops**. In taxis, sit in the backseat, unless that's where the driver is, in which case consider taking a bus.

Traveller's Tip

Women should avoid wearing white. This has nothing to do with security – it just makes you look fat.

Travellers with Disabilities

Unfortunately, San Sombrèro is not well equipped for people with disabilities. Cobblestone streets, **steep trails** and uneven pavements, coupled with the local tendency to ridicule anyone who can't dance, make **wheelchair travel** somewhat difficult. Probably the best way for people with disabilities to experience the **magic** of San Sombrèro is to send an **able-bodied friend** with a good video camera. That said, things are improving, with several up-market hotels now catering for guests with low level **handicaps**, such as insomnia and bucked teeth.

Gay & Lesbian Travellers

As a predominantly **Catholic** country, San Sombrèro is not overly tolerant of **homosexuality**, except of course within its clergy, and harassment is common. One of the worst instances took place last year when several floats in a **gay pride** rally were car-jacked. Also, avoid any behaviour that might be seen by San Sombrèrans as overly 'gay', such using a **pedestrian crossing** or ordering decaffeinated coffee.

Traveller's Tip

You'll often see men walking down the street arm in arm – this gesture has no sexual meaning, unless one of them is wearing leather pants.

Each April members of San Sombrèro's gay community are proudly marched through town and into the nearest jail.

When to Go

Apart from September to November (**prime hurricane months**), July and August (when **ferocious heat** makes touring unpleasant), and December to April (the rainforest burning-off period), pretty much **anytime of the year** is good for a visit to San Sombrèro. However, the wet season is best avoided because the heat can be intense and many roads impassable. June is considered a better option as the clouds of stinging hornets will often provide **partial shade** from the sun's rays.

Travelling off-season is, of course, cheaper, although you should be prepared for the possibility of prolonged **rains**, high winds, frequent power outages and little being open. Along the east coast in October it can also be difficult to find a **hotel**, as many of them will have been blown away by **hurricanes**.

Philippe Writes... For the Serious Traveller
I scoff at the concept of an 'off-season'. What's a little rain or the occasional storm if it means you can enjoy a destination free of hapless holidaymakers? My best ever trip to San Sombrèro was one October when I got to spend three weeks huddling in a flooded underground hurricane shelter fearing for my life.

During the normally quiet hurricane season many hotels in San Sombrèro will have rooms. Unfortunately, very few will have roofs.

Special Events & Festivals

From parades and **pilgrimages** to rodeos and colourful *tiroteos* (public executions), just about every month in San Sombrèro includes a **festival** of some sort. Many are linked to the Roman Catholic calendar, with Easter easily being the biggest **holiday** of the year, although November's **Monster Truck Parade** comes a close second.

While Carnivale is perhaps the most widely known of San Sombrèro's **festivals**, it doesn't take much for spontaneous celebrations to break out; a local saint's **birthday**, a sporting victory, the arrest of another government minister – all can lead to a party. **Traditional dances** and music form an essential part of most events, along with a **procession** behind some revered holy image or logo belonging to a major sponsor.

Note *As a general rule, San Sombrèrans are not very good on dates. Thus, the day before Remembrance Day is known as Reminder for Remembrance Day Day. Also, precise dates may often vary – don't be surprised if May Day celebrations actually take place in July.*

5 January San Nicotiño Day. Celebrations honouring this much-loved saint also mark the start of Emphysema Awareness Week.

28 January Independence Day. Citizens of Cucarucha City will gather in the Plaza del Popolo for speeches and **patriotic songs**, capped off by a march on the Presidential Palace and, in particularly rowdy years, a coup.

29 January Dependence Day. Celebrations marking San Sombrèro's continued reliance on overseas aid.

February Carnivale is celebrated throughout the Roman Catholic world. In San Sombrèro it involves a wild two-week party during which **locals** take their pleasure before undertaking the forty-minute abstinence of Lent.

12 March Anniversary of the **Constitution**.

13 March Anniversary of the **Overthrow of the Constitution**.

April During Easter week (Thursday–Sunday) most of the country shuts down with just essential services such as hospitals and **casinos** remaining open. A series of masses, processions and parades take place throughout the country, along with the annual draw of **Madonna-Lotto**.

2 May **National Day of Unity** (only in the south).

22 May **Rumfest** celebrates the introduction of rum to the country with a weekend of parties, dancing, parades and an amnesty for anyone caught drink driving.

5–7 July **Fiesta del Maiz** (Corn Festival). Residents dressed in costumes made entirely of corn parade down the street, after which a **Corn Queen** is named and then eaten.

6 August **National Women's Day** (Dia de las Mujeres) celebrates the rights and achievements of San Sombrèran women.

7 August The **Miss San Sombrèro Pageant** makes them walk around in swimsuits.

1–3 September **The Fiesta de Café** (Coffee Festival) in the Central Valley celebrates the harvest with a week long coffee-picking contest. (This is not an 'official' event – it was dreamt up by **plantation owners** as a way of getting gullible backpackers to harvest their crop for free.)

2 November **Dia de los Muertos** (Day of the Dead) is observed nationwide with special church services and families robbing each other's graves. To honour their dead relatives it used to be customary for people to build **shrines** in their backyards but more often these days the holiday is used to construct barbecues or patio extensions.

1 December **Benito Juara Day**. Held in the colonial city of Acuna, this feast day commemorates wealthy local **businessman** Benita Juara who has never actually done anything of note, but pays the equivalent of US$2 million each year for the privilege of being thus honoured.

Members of San Sombrèro's Despotic Youth League prepare to march.

Getting There

San Sombrèro's **national carrier** is Aero Sombrèro, which celebrated its 50th anniversary last year with a major **re-fit** of its entire fleet, along with an oil change. Aero Sombrèro offers a generally good service although some concerns have been raised regarding **safety standards**. These relate specifically to **crew levels**, with several passengers expressing concern that the co-pilot was required to serve **beverages** during the flight.

Another option is Aero Reliable (or, as it is known in aviation circles, Air Mayday), a **budget carrier** boasting one of the oldest and most frequently **repaired** fleets in the world. Ticket prices are generally low, with further **discounts** available for passengers prepared to sit in the **toilets** or help start the propeller. Some flights even have a **First Class** (*Clase Tropical*) section with extra leg-room gained by doing away with lifejackets.

> **Note** *Several San Sombrèran air carriers boast a Business Class section where passengers can lie flat. In many cases this will involve a hammock.*

All Aero Sombrèro craft are regularly serviced. Those deemed beyond repair are converted into buses, or used for joy flights.

Helena Writes...
For the Eco-Traveller
We all know that airlines cause immense amounts of pollution, however a new company, Green-Air, has been experimenting with engines that run on low octane, lead-free aviation fuel. It's early days, but results collected so far from the black box flight data recorders used by their test aircraft have been very encouraging.

By Car

Taking your own car into San Sombrèro will obviously give you a great deal more options. Should your **accommodation** fall through, for example, you'll have somewhere to sleep. But there are complications, such as the **state of local roads** with most being generally poor and potholed. (Even San Sombrèro's 'superhighways' are frequently blocked by wandering **cattle**, so much so that the government is considering building a livestock lane.)

Getting Around

San Sombrèro is deceptively **large** – about the size of Texas (coincidentally, it executes the same number of prisoners each year) – which makes **getting round** the entire country no easy task. For many people, the easiest way is to take an **organised tour**. However, this often means travelling with other tourists, something that can greatly limit your overall **enjoyment**, especially if they're members of your own family.

By Air

The fastest way to get around is to fly. Unfortunately, San Sombrèro's internal air network is somewhat disorganised. There are four **domestic carriers**, although two of these are reserved for **freight** and the third used exclusively to transport livestock, leaving just one, Aviacon Sombrèro, for tourists. Most of the Aviacon Sombrèro fleet is made up of former **Russian** military aircraft, such as Antonov-26's and Yak-40's so don't expect much in the way of **in-flight comfort**, unless you're lucky enough to be seated in one of the rear-gun turrets.

By Car

San Sombrèro has some 27,000km of roads, of which about 15,500km are potholes. Whilst the cities can be **congested**, once in the countryside the traffic thins; in parts you can travel all day and sometimes pass only a dozen **vehicles**, many of which will be in a ditch or on fire. To drive in San Sombrèro you must be at least 21 years of age, have a **driver's licence** and a legally binding will.

Due to fuel shortages, in many San Sombrèran cities it is illegal to operate a motorbike with less than three passengers.

Taxis are generally quite cheap. However, in larger cities drivers will charge an extra 10 cents each time they use the brakes.

On the Road

Sadly, **traffic deaths** are common and San Sombrèran highways feature more roadside **shrines** to automobile accident victims than anywhere else in the world. The situation has got so out of hand that on certain dangerous **corners** families have to book space years in advance.

Unfortunately San Sombrèro does not have a national **ambulance service** so, in the event of witnessing an accident, the best you can do is call a local **doctor** or police. If the accident is particularly bad you might consider calling the **United Nations**. One of the main cause of traffic deaths in San Sombrèro is collisions with wayward **livestock**. Compulsory road safety education courses were trialled some years back, but the country's **cattle** refused to attend.

It's a good idea to carry an **international driving licence** with your photo clearly displayed on the front and a US $20 note loosely attached to the back. Finding fuel is generally not a problem, as both **service stations** and **ruptured oil pipelines** are easy to spot. In an emergency most **bars** will sell you a locally made rum more than capable of powering the average engine.

A cyclist searches for his bike, lost down a pot-hole.

Traveller's Tip

Motorists from developed countries should remember that the San Sombrèran highway system is not governed by strict road rules, drink-driving laws, or – for that matter – the Geneva Convention.

WHAT'S IN A NAME?

One of the great difficulties in finding your way round San Sombrèro's larger cities is the fact that so many of its streets and avenues are named after recent political or public figures. Whenever there is a change in leadership or popularity every one of these thoroughfares must then be renamed. Hence, a major east–west thoroughfare in Cucaracha City has, over the past decade, been known as Avenida San Rafael, Avenida Popolo, Avenida General Juan Perez and Avenida Ricky Martin.

¡Viva El Jalopo!

The unofficial 'national car' of San Sombrèro would have to be the ubiquitous *El Jalopo*. It seems that just about everyone in the country has owned one, driven one, been hit by one or conceived on the back seat of one. Modelled on the Ford Oldsmobile (though designed to look older) this grand old dame of the road is made out of cast iron and lead, and features such luxuries as a marble dashboard. While this added weight reduces fuel economy, it does make the *El Jalopo* an excellent place to shelter during severe hurricanes.

In many parts of San Sombrèro it is considered 'unmanly' to actually travel inside a vehicle. (Even on short air flights passengers have been known to demand a seat on the wing.)

Buses

There are a multitude of bus companies operating throughout San Sombrèro, and **competition** between them can often get quite intense. Stories of sabotage and **rival drivers** trying to run each other off the road may be a little exaggerated but it is worth booking a service with **bulletproof glass**. Fortunately, the legendary craziness of San Sombrèran bus drivers is largely a thing of the past, and many bus companies have installed **warning lights** or **buzzers** to indicate when the driver is speeding or asleep.

There are basically two classes of bus, first (*primera*) and second (*tractore*). First-class buses offer **reserved seating**, videos and air-conditioning. However, it should be mentioned that many of the videos are not exactly suitable **family viewing** as many contain scenes of scantily-clad women. If possible, distract your little ones by having them look out the **window**, at real scenes of scantily-clad women.

San Sombrèrans relinquish their seats readily to the elderly, **pregnant women**, disabled passengers and members of the **military**. Those travelling with young children or mysterious **packages** will also get preferential treatment.

Rail

Two major **rail links** cross the country, the north line that runs north–south and the east line that doesn't run at all.

The Rolling Stones left San Sombrèro long ago, but their old tour bus is still being put to good use.

Money

San Sombrèro's national unit of currency is the *crapeso*. There are 100 *cachingos* to each crapeso. The crapeso replaces earlier **currencies** such as the *plectro* and, before that, the *conch*. **Banknotes** are easy to distinguish from each other as they come in different sizes, colours and **smell**. For example, the green one-crapeso note is a little nutty.

Banks

Banking hours are generally 8am to 3pm, although most close for an hour for **lunch** and to arrest staff caught stealing during the **morning shift**. There are ATMs in most of the larger cities; however, these **machines** frequently run out of money in which event you will be issued with a formal I.O.U.

SAN SOMBRERO INDICES	CRAPESO (C)	USD($)	BARTER
SSSX All	4813.80	74.24	
SSSX MIDCAP 50	4483.66	72.13	
SSSX MATERIALS	3985.10	65.20	
SSSX INDUSTRIALS	4680.33	72.62	
SSSX FINANCIALS	4100.75	68.23	
SSSX TELCO SERVS	4269.22	70.24	
BVSP TOTAL FUTURES	4155.22	68.99	
MXX TOTAL OPTIONS	4023.62	77.32	
MERV BOND YIELD	4723.57	73.82	

San Sombrèro has one of the few stock exchanges to permit bartering. Daily listings are published in crapesos, US dollars and their livestock equivalent.

The Print Media

Most newspapers in San Sombrèro are rather lurid scandal sheets, often brimming with violent crime depicted in **full colour**. The nation's official paper is *El Propagando*, a daily journal shamelessly devoted to the **achievements** and wise economic stewardship of the **president**. All sections of the paper reflect this theme, even the horoscopes, with typical entries such as:

> *'Aquarius. A positive change is due, much like the positive economic reforms currently being instigated by the government…'*

Some attempts have been made in recent years to balance this approach and *El Propagando* now even features the **occasional article** critical of the president, along with an in-depth **obituary** of the journalist who wrote it.

Examples of the tabloid La Sensacional's *unique headline style, including the moon landing, Pope's death and Kennedy Assasination.*

Communications Telephones

The telephone is the most widespread **system of communication** in San Sombrèro, except in the south, where **smoke-signals** remain the preferred method.

Be warned – when phoning from a hotel various **surcharges** may often be added, making the cost of the **call** quite high. If the person you plan on calling actually lives within San Sombrèro it may be **cheaper** to drive over and have the conversation in person.

International calls, too, can be outrageously expensive. The cheapest way to communicate is via '**operator-assisted**' calls; here you do not actually speak directly to the person you are calling, instead you speak with an **operator** who will then – hopefully – pass on your message.

Reverse-charge or 'collect' calls (*por cobrar*) are another **economic means** of making contact outside of San Sombrèro. The operator will generally ask you the name and number of the person you are calling, the **number** you are calling from, your name and whether you are married or interested in a long-term **relationship**. Call rates will vary depending upon your answer to this last question.

If you wish to use a **cell** (mobile) phone in San Sombrèro, check with your **provider** whether it will work there. Coverage, especially in **outlying** areas, is limited by the tendency for **flocks of parakeets** to nest in communication towers.

Phone books in San Sombrèro list people, not in alphabetical order, but according to perceived social status. Thus, government ministers, celebrities, successful businessmen and anyone related to a member of the national soccer team will appear first, followed by less 'esteemed' subscribers such as criminals, bankrupts, alcoholics, the unemployed, lawyers and homosexuals.

Public phone booths are plentiful through-out San Sombrèro; however, during the day many are used as childcare centres.

Mail

Sending **packages** out of the country is drowned in bureaucracy, with **regulations** governing everything from the thickness of brown **paper** to the amount of string that may legally be used. In some cases even **letters** will be opened and scrutinised for punctuation and grammar.

Tina Writes...
For the Cautious Traveller
When buying goods overseas, never fall for an offer to ship your purchase home. It simply will not happen. If something I've bought needs to be mailed, I insist on having myself wrapped and placed in the crate with it.

Email & the Internet

The internet is booming in San Sombrèro and there are plenty of internet **cafés** and public access facilities to be found. The only **downside** is that the government imposes quite **rigid filtering**, and any reference to politics, civil liberties, military exercises or the president's **hair loss** will see your connection instantly terminated and the café **raided** by local police.

Philippe Writes...
I scoff at tourists constantly checking their email at internet cafés, desperate to stay in touch with home. When I leave on a trip I tell my family and friends that they won't be hearing from me for months. And you know what? They've *never* complained.

Internet connection speeds are so slow in San Sombrèro that it is often quicker to unplug your computer and deliver its hard drive in person.

Accommodation

San Sombrèro offers a wide choice of accommodation **options**, ranging from exclusive **boutique hotels** through to underground hovels so dilapidated that even the long-term **homeless** will refuse to sleep in them.

A few unique features worth noting:

- All rooms should have a prominent sign displaying **official prices**. Do not move this – it is probably covering a hole in the wall.

- Remember, in most San Sombrèran hotels a 'double bed' will consist of two **single beds** pushed together. You can request a 'matrimonial bed', which consists of two single beds pushed apart.

- Bathplugs are often **stolen** from San Sombrèran hotels, especially in the north where they are considered **legal currency**.

- In many hotels guests will find a **newspaper** slid under their door each morning. This is not for reading – it's toilet tissue.

Traveller's Tip

In bathrooms 'C' stands for *caliente*, meaning hot, not cold. Fortunately, very few visitors have ever been scalded as the water in hotels is rarely ever hot.

In top-end establishments fresh linen will be folded into an impressive range of animal shapes. In budget hotels it's more likely to be dumped on the floor.

At the lower level, accommodation prices are often based on how much of your hotel room's balcony is missing.

02 San Sombrèro
CUCARACHA CITY

Introduction

Considered one of the most **beautiful** and beguiling of all Central American cities, San Sombrèro's capital sits, like a **grand old colonial dame**, basking on the shores of Merinda Bay. The political, cultural and industrial **heart** of San Sombrèro, Cucaracha City contains one-fifth of the country's **population** (both human and rodent) as well as most of its wealth.

A place of **leisurely walks** – especially when your promised free hotel transfer bus fails to show up – here the blues and oranges of ornate Spanish **villas** sit side-by-side with the grey of modern **industrial estates**. It's no surprise, then, that Cucaracha City was recently voted one of the world's **Most Squattable** Cities.

There are quiet museums, cobblestone pedestrian boulevards and **shady inner-city parks** where groups of elderly men can be seen enjoying a friendly game of *cardillo* (strip-poker). Many of the city's older **streets** are lined with grand, colonial-era houses, their **balconies** sporting colourful pots of *cacarnia*, a hardy plant that can survive high pollution levels, limited sunlight and general **neglect** – as can the citizens of this bustling urban centre.

For many, the city's **harbour** is one of its feature attractions, and a stroll along the waterfront shops and cafés of *Passo de Agua* is a must. One word of **warning** – be prepared to get wet! If not from the odd **wave**, then from the many high rise construction workers for whom spitting would seem to be an almost **religious ritual**.

Cars break down with such frequency in Cucaracha City that many bonnets have rusted permanently open.

You can buy just about anything on the streets of Cucaracha City, from (clockwise from top left) freshly grown vegetables and flowers, to freshly poached eggs and wildlife.

Despite the noise and chaos, Cucaracha City remains a relatively **safe place**. Very few residents here even bother locking their **doors**, as most of these locks have long ago been stolen – along with their doors. Of course, there are sections of the city worth avoiding. The most notorious, in terms of **danger**, is the *barrio* (neighbourhood) of Otarya, a district so plagued by street violence that its **borders** are permanently marked by tape bearing the words 'Police Crime Scene – Do Not Cross'. The most historically significant district is *barrio* Lagua, **home** to some of the city's oldest colonial mansions and churches as well as, of course, the city's magnificent **Presidential Palace**. Here visitors flock to catch a glimpse of San Sombrèro's famous Changing of the Guard. This ceremonial event takes place once a week to coincide with the Changing of the Government.

For those less interested in **old world attractions**, the riverfront *barrio* of Callecon is *the* place to wine, dine and dance the night away. Once Cucaracha City's most **desirable district**, the wealthy moved away en masse when **yellow fever** hit during the 1870s. Residents were prompted to make a similar move a century later when **disco fever** hit, with noisy dance venues drawing revellers from around the world.

Despite its **historical charm**, Cucaracha City is also a modern centre very much on the move. New office blocks are going up, roads are being built and ancient native **burial grounds** are getting converted into housing estates at a furious rate. Of course, this endless pursuit of **progress** has come at a cost. Cucaracha City's new public hospital was so hastily built that by the time of its official opening in 2004 an entire ward was filled solely with **injured** construction workers.

Members of the Presidential Guard prepare to celebrate their country's latest coup.

Traveller's Tip

In downtown Cucaracha City, street names are generally displayed on little plaques attached to the sides of either a corner building or the guitar case of a regular busker.

Finding Your Way Round

San Sombrèro's capital is laid out on a **grid** – *avenidas* (avenues) run north–south and *calles* (streets) run east–west. That's the easy part. Unfortunately, Cucarachans do not use **street numbers**, relying instead on an archaic system that makes sense to them but can confuse visitors. A typical Cucaracha City **address** might be '200m north and 50m east of the post office' – not too bad except for the fact that the **post office** in question may or may not still exist.

Then there are the somewhat more colloquial (therefore less obvious) points of **geographic reference**. You could, for example, be told your hotel is '100m south and 50m east of the **spot** Isabel slapped Miguel'.

Traveller's Tip

In Cucaracha City life is relaxed, and everything runs to 'rubber time'. Get used to the fact your 7.30am wake-up call might not come 'til midday, or a shop with a door sign reading 'back in five minutes' might not reopen until summer. Embrace it, go with it. Nothing moves quickly in San Sombrèro, with the curious exception of elevator doors that often seem to slam shut with alarming speed.

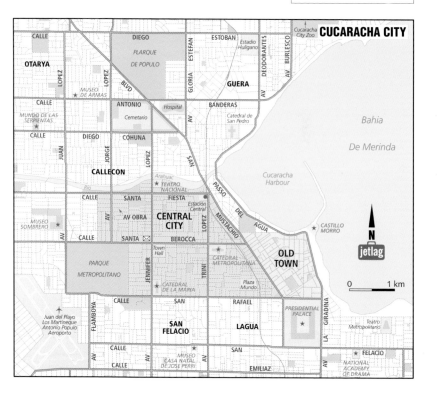

History

When Spanish **settlers** first landed and began exploring the area around Merinda Bay they expected to find great **cities** and monuments typical of Meso-America. Instead, they found a small population of **hunter-gatherers** living in trees. Unlike the neighbouring Incas and Mayans, the region's original indigenous people never developed a highly advanced **civilisation**. There is some evidence that, around 3000BC, they mastered **fire** but it appears to have then taken them another 500 years to devise a safe **method** of putting it out. By the 5th century this tribe died out, as did most of the grasslands around them, leaving the plains along San Sombrèro's west coast largely inhabited by the Arahuac, a **peaceful tribe** who survived by **fishing** and hiring themselves out as human sacrifices. Their staple diet was **shellfish**, which they would catch and dry along the beach; the flesh kept them nourished and the smell **repelled** most invaders.

But in 1509 this **blissful existence** was shattered when the Spanish explorer, Diegos Estoban, who was sailing up the west coast of San Sombrèro, came ashore to go to the toilet. To his **surprise**, Estoban discovered a pleasant, deep water harbour and friendly people. 'There were about 50 men and over 200 women, **brown-skinned**, all of them naked, without anything to cover their private parts' he wrote in his **diary**, before resigning as captain and announcing his intention to live with the natives.

Early attempts by the Spanish to establish a permanent settlement in Cucaracha were not overly successful. Several rough **huts** were erected along the shore of Merinda Bay but the **combination** of mosquitos, constant winds and native dance ceremonies made life unbearable for the early settlers. A senior **officer**, Colonel Emiliaz, was sent to scout for alternative locations, returning some months later to say he knew of a more **promising site**. Unfortunately this turned out to be in Madrid, and the settlers were forced to stay.

Given its strategic position, Cucaracha City soon came **under attack** from other countries such as Portugal and France, as well as **pirate gangs** eager to plunder the settlement. Early efforts at protecting the city during the 16th century revolved around building an impressive network of fortresses. These had **limited value** as they were generally made of **mud** and all invading navies had to do was wait for rain.

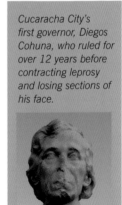

Cucaracha City's first governor, Diegos Cohuna, who ruled for over 12 years before contracting leprosy and losing sections of his face.

Nevertheless by the 17th century Cucaracha City was a **thriving port**, with a population of around 20,000, an incredible third of whom were priests. Charged with spreading the word of God, these **missionaries** set about converting the native population with ferocious zeal. Compulsory **baptisms** and bible study classes were the norm, and anyone who refused to embrace Catholicism was imprisoned, or forced to attend church **organ** recitals.

By the start of the 19th century the people of Cucaracha were tiring of Spanish rule. Taxation without representation was **a major source of irritation**, as was the widespread use of **castanets**. Various half-hearted attempts to overthrow the colonial government were brutally put down by military force. In 1836 a Cucarachan-born merchant named Jean Marquez staged an **uprising**, taking over the Town Hall, where he called for his co-revolutionaries to join him in singing the San Sombrèran national **anthem**. At this point it was realised they didn't actually have one, and the next hour was spent arguing round a **piano**, by which time government forces were able to recapture the building.

Over the coming **decades** further challenges to the colonial government took place with increasing frequency. In 1852, one of the city's most **famous** independence leaders, Raul Calle, openly called for an end to imperial rule, a move that saw him immediately **jailed**. Calle then went on a much-publicised **hunger strike** which, whilst unsuccessful in overthrowing the **government**, did allow him to lose so much **weight** that he was able to slip out between the bars of his prison cell and finally lead a successful revolt.

On 6 January 1853, independence was granted and Calle passionately declared 'Today is the day Cucaracha City finally woke up', before **retiring** for his daily siesta.

Dating back to the first century AD, these native ruins are believed to be one of the first basketball courts ever built. Note the stone ball [left].

Getting There
By Plane

International passengers arrive at Juan del Playo Los Martineque del Pueblo Aeroporto, one of the few international **airports** whose name does not actually fit on the **terminal building**. The airport is very much within city limits and as you come in to land you get amazing views of the **city** below, unless your window is blocked by a cabin attendant checking that the **undercarriage** has locked into place. The airport itself is modern and boasts a **non-smoking lounge**, as well as a prayer room, often filled with nervous passengers and, disturbingly, flight **maintenance** crews.

Because of strong ocean winds, flights into Cucaracha City often experience **severe turbulence**. While the sudden bumps and dips can be uncomfortable, they do have the **advantage** of keeping the pilot awake.

Most visitors arrive on flights operated by Aero Sombrèro, an airline that has **worked hard** in recent years to raise **safety standards**. After numerous near mid-air collisions, it's entire fleet has recently been fitted with **nudge bars** and very loud horns. For visitors coming from the United States, Aero Sombrèro operates daily flights from Miami to Cucaracha City that take about an hour or so, depending on **winds** and whether or not they bother with the safety talk.

Customs officers at Cucaracha City airport use trained **security dogs** to sniff out contraband. If something suspect is detected there'll usually be a series of excited 'yelps', either from the **dog** or its handler realising how much he is likely to get for this find on the black market.

TOP TOUTS!
Cucaracha City's airport boasts some of the most aggressive touts in the country, all pushing for you to ride in their taxi, stay at their hotel or book for one of their tours. Arriving passengers have even reported being accosted by the San Sombrèran Immigration Minister himself, who is apparently paid on a commission basis.

SAFETY FIRST
Due to increased **security concerns** travellers checking in may be required to remove their belts and shoes. It is not, however, necessary to remove underwear and female passengers being asked to do so should report the matter to airport staff.

A lack of plumbing has not stopped many home owners installing an upstairs bathroom.

Getting Around

For all its size and **frantic pace**, once you're used to it, Cucaracha City is surprisingly easy to get around, whether by bus, cab, private car or in the back of an **ambulance**. As a general rule, you'll save a lot of hassle if you avoid travelling during **rush hour** (generally between 1am and 3am when people are heading home from night clubs).

Rental Car

Renting a car can be an excellent way of getting round Cucaracha City, although many find **driving** something of a 'challenge'. Locals rarely stop at **red lights** as many of these have been installed by resourceful street vendors keen to make a **sale**. Remember, too, that road signs tend not always to be strictly for safety purposes. Don't be **surprised** to see signs such 'Slow Down – Cheap Jackets Ahead' or 'Stop – It's Time for a Beer'.

Wandering livestock can present a major hazard on all San Sombrèran roads and Cucaracha City is no exception. Drivers should be particularly **wary** of cows and horses, especially if these animals are behind the wheel of a car.

There are numerous car **rental agencies** in Cucaracha City; if they don't have the type of vehicle you want, an obliging staff member will happily go outside and **car-jack** one for you (additional costs and criminal charges may apply).

There is also a government run **Tourist Information** office in the centre of town that stocks a large range of street maps. Curiously, none are of Cucaracha City. The staff seem to have taken the **slogan** 'Central America's best-kept secret' literally.

A must-see sight in Cucaracha City is its brightly uniformed traffic cops [left] who stand in the middle of **intersections** gyrating, swivelling and gesticulating at passing traffic. Motorists are welcome to ask them for directions or, for a **small tip**, to re-enact a scene from *Footloose*.

San Sombrèro leads the world in production of ethanol, a sugar-based fuel regularly used in cars and motorbikes, as well as certain cocktails.

Buses

Cucaracha City's buses are often described as being full of 'local colour', often a reference to the fact that someone has **thrown up** in the back seats. That said, buses can be a good (and cheap) way of getting round, provided you remember **a few tips**. The city displayed on the front of a bus is often not its **destination** but, in fact, the **birthplace** of the driver. Some older-style buses are entered from the rear and once used an honour system of passing your **coins** forward is employed. This was abandoned some years ago after passengers involved in the process began claiming a commission.

Just finally, don't be surprised if the bus you've hailed fails to **stop**; it's either full, or it's **brakes** have just failed.

Modern traffic signals in Cucaracha City not only indicate when it is safe to cross, but also the number of pedestrians struck by cars that week.

By Taxi

Once chaotic, Cucaracha City's taxi industry has recently been regulated, with all prospective drivers now expected to complete a **written exam** and have reached at least level three on *Grand Theft Auto*. Generally there are two **categories** of driver: sober and drunk.

The most common (and **cheapest**) form of taxi you'll see round the city is a *taxi colectivo*. These are not recommended for **tourists**, as drivers will pack as many people into the car as possible and often refuse to set off until even the trunk, **roof-rack** and cup-holders are full. **Metered taxis** are a little more expensive but you will have the luxury of your own seat and, possibly, some form of suspension system. Always insist that the driver switches his **meter** on (a small fee may apply for this service).

In theory Cucaracha City taxi **drivers** do not require a tip. However, most have come to expect one, and the **local industry** is one of the few in the world to routinely charge a departure tax.

CUCARACHA CITY BY AIR

Aero Viva is a small company that offers scenic flights over the city in their twin-seater biplanes. These trips are a real thrill, not just for passengers but also the pilots, many off whom are making their first flight without an instructor.

Plagues of stinging insects in the Port District of Cucaracha City are so bad that entire buildings need to be covered in mosquito nets.

Shopping

While the range of **consumer products** available for purchase in Cucaracha City is expanding, the quality and choice is generally poor, unless – of course – you're after **carved coconut figurines** or low-grade rum.

Several larger department stores in Cucaracha City stay **open past midnight**, however, for security reasons, most are cleared of all merchandise, making a late-night shopping expedition theoretically possible but technically pointless.

Socially aware shoppers should keep an eye out for Sombrer-Ex stores, featuring products made by **underprivileged youths** and the unemployed. These outlets are run by a **non-profit organisation** and, given the quality of goods on offer, this status is unlikely to change.

Tina Writes...
For the Cautious Traveller
When carrying valuables keep them out of sight under your clothes. In fact, keep your clothes (another popular target for thieves) out of sight under a set of decoy clothes or – better still – travel semi-nude, thus cutting off any chance of having a valuable pair of jeans or favourite shirt stolen.

Counterfeit handbags are a popular item for shoppers in Cucaracha City. Here you can get reproductions of big brand names such as Louis Vuitton, Fendi and Prada, which are indistinguishable from the real thing, apart from the fact they're made of straw.

Where to Stay

There is no shortage of accommodation in Cucaracha City, ranging from **budget** hostels through to hip, up-market **boutique** hotels. In some parts of the city electricity supplies are somewhat erratic meaning that ceiling fans and bedside lamps should be considered as purely **decorative**. As for facilities, remember that the term 'bathroom' generally means a toilet, washbasin and shower, although in some **cheaper establishments** don't be surprised if these three utilities are actually combined.

Of course, when it comes to **rating** accommodation, standards and definitions do vary – there's a fine line between a **skylight** and a hole in the roof. In this guide we've **ranked** hotels as Expensive, Mid-Range and Budget.

🌂🌂🌂 Expensive

✉ 96 Av Jennifer Lopez
☎ 37 889 259
@ villa@sombrero.com.ss
▤ MC V

Villa Sombrèro This classic 19th-century hotel in a superb location on the lively Parque Central is considered *the* place to stay in Cucaracha City. Guests are greeted with freshly cut flowers, and elevator music is provided live by vocal groups who travel between floors.

✉ 330 Blvd San Mustachio
☎ 37 887 544
@ montero@hostal .com.ss
▤ DC

Hostal Montero, a stylishly artistic 1920s hotel in the centre of town that features an original metal cage elevator so slow that passengers ascending in it may be at risk from deep vein thrombosis. Suites on the top floor boast fabulous views of the city square and Presidential Palace. Popular with both top-end travellers and rebel snipers.

✉ 668 Calle Santa Fiesta
☎ 37 775 218
@ nacional@hostale.com.ss
▤ MC

Hostal Nacional The perennially popular Nacional was built in 1850 but has recently been given a facelift, as has its owner Senorita Lopez.

MASSAGE

A range of massage therapies are offered at many of the larger hotels in Cucaracha City, ranging from traditional massage, which draws upon techniques perfected during the Spanish Inquisition through to treatments such as express rub-downs, designed for business travellers with only a limited time scheduled for relaxing. In most cases you'll be offered the option of 'aromatherapy' which means, for a small additional fee, your masseuse will agree to wear deodorant.

J. Despite being one of Cucaracha City's hippest new hotels, the J. is not easy to locate as there are no signs outside and guests must find their way into the lobby by pushing against the correct glass panel. Staff members here are all young and good-looking (breaking out in acne is considered a sackable offence) and guests over 30 may be charged an old-age levy.

✉ *2 Calle Antonio Banderas*
☎ *37 852 1648*
@ *thej@j.com.ss*
▤ *MC V*

The Riviera is another of Cucaracha City's up-market hotels. Popular with business travellers, the Riviera has recently installed a self-service electronic check-in system; however, several guests registering have reported problems with this facility, such as being issued with a key to a room that's already occupied, yet to be cleaned or actually in another hotel. Others have simply been electrocuted.

✉ *78 Av Trini Lopez*
☎ *37 879 558*
@ *riviera@cuca.com.ss*
▤ *V MC DC*

Traveller's Tip 👍

Upon checking in to many of Cucaracha City's up-market hotels you may find a bottle of rum, along with a note from the manager welcoming you. Many guests drink the bottle, assuming it to be complimentary. It is not and you will be charged for the bottle, as well as a small fee for the letter.

Swim-up bars such as this one boast an extensive range of chlorinated cocktails.

☁☁ Mid-Range

☒ *88 Av Gloria Estefan*
☎ *37 855 258*
@ *plaza@arron.com.ss*

Arron Plaza A good choice for those seeking a large hotel with local flavour, the Arron takes pride in the fact that every one of their 90-plus rooms is slightly different, the result of a recent earthquake that has left various forms of structural damage throughout the building.

☒ *67 Calle San Felacio*
☎ *37 225 981*
@ *hostal@teconde.com.ss*
▤ *V MC DC*
  courtyard

Hostal Teconde This stately 17th-century home was built around an ornately tiled courtyard. The subsequent owners neglected, however, to install drains and the courtyard could now more accurately be described as a shallow pool.

☒ *900 Av Juan Lopez*
☎ *37 986 968*
@ *bruz@hostal.com.ss*
  showers
  'rooftop garden'

Hostal Bruzon A private home-turned-hotel, the Bruzon is run by two brothers who are both currently serving home detention sentences. All rooms boast showers although, should any other guest in the hotel be using theirs, you won't get much in the way of water pressure. Rumours circulating on certain travel websites about a 'rooftop garden' actually refer to a hydroponic plant nursery hidden in the attic, and are best not mentioned.

☒ *85 Calle Diego Cohuna*
☎ *37 226 496*
@ *turistico@hostal.com.ss*

Hostal Turistico This locally owned pensione gets excellent reviews from guests, often as a condition of having their passport returned. Rooms are best described as 'atmospheric' (very few of the windows actually shut) and are carpeted throughout, including – somewhat unusually – the shower cubicle.

☒ *5 Calle Diego Estoban*
☎ *37 885 976*
@ *cabana@inn.com.ss*
▤ *V MC DC*
  courtyard

Cabana Inn Situated in the waterfront section of town, the stylish Cabana Inn offers 'partial ocean views', meaning that during severe hurricanes the apartment block in front may sway just far enough to offer a glimpse of the nearby harbour. The hotel's large communal spa is popular with both guests and mosquito larvae.

☁ Budget

Casa Hidalgo This simple but attractive hotel is run by a local resident, Senora Hidalgo. Its rooms are pleasant, with welcome touches in the form of woodblock prints on the walls, as well as not-so-welcome touches in the form of groping from Senor Hidalgo who can often be seen in the lobby 'welcoming' female guests.

✉ *9990 Passo del Agua*
☎ *37 846 259*
@ *casa@miguel.com.ss*
🖃 *V MC*

Pencion Capri One of the city's most popular budget options, the Capri's basic rooms are a little cramped – if you plan on opening the mini-bar fridge it may be necessary to move the bed. Those wanting a little more space might opt for one of their deluxe rooms, which has two beds, although during peak season one of these may be occupied by a member of staff.

✉ *74 Calle San Rafael*
☎ *37 226 874*
@ *capri@hostal.com.ss*
    mini bar

Casa Marta A private first floor apartment offering several basic rooms with ceiling fans and small balconies. None have TV but, as the owners live downstairs, you can generally count on hearing their set most hours of the day.

✉ *9 Av La Giradina*
☎ *37 002 986*
@ *marta@marta.com.ss*
🖃 *V*

La Cucaracha Considered *the* place for backpackers, this four-storey establishment offers accommodation to suit just about every level of shoe-string budget. Beds on the ground floor are in little compartments with doors – a dormitory on the second floor offers bunks – the third floor has one large communal mattress and the fourth floor is best not described.

✉ *76 Passo del Aqua*
☎ *37 963 581*
@ *la@cucaracha.com.ss*
    communal mattress

Cucaracha City's most famous 'Love Hotel', the somewhat seedy old El Prostico, offers romantic extras such as waterbeds and jacuzzis. However, guests should be warned that the 'Adult Channel' advertised in the hotel's brochure is, in fact, merely a direct CCTV feed from the honeymoon suite.

Where to Eat

While Cucaracha City might not rank as one of the world's great culinary capitals, it is possible to eat well here. Many **exciting new bistros**, bars and restaurants have opened up in recent years and the competition between them has led to a noticeable rise in both quality and the incidence of mysterious fire-bombings.

The choice of where to eat is almost limitless in Cucaracha City. In the centre of the old city you'll find dozens of **small cafés** (*cafettas*) and humble street stalls (*dysenteria*) serving authentic local fare. Those seeking a more sophisticated dining experience (one with cutlery) might consider eating at one of the larger hotels.

Most meals in San Sombrèro will be accompanied by a bottle of rum. This versatile spirit can be enjoyed with mixers as a **refreshing pre-dinner drink**, or drunk 'straight' during main course. Sweet rum tends to be served with dessert as a *digestif* and anything left in the bottle will be used after you've left to polish the table.

Traveller's Tip

When ordering rum, ask for a 'Septo' – one that has been aged for at least seven days.

☁☁☁ Expensive

✉ *88 Calle Santa Berocca*
☎ *37 880 570*
@ *aqua@rius.com.ss*
▭ *V DC MC*

Aquarius One of Cucaracha City's signature dining establishments, this sumptuous seafood restaurant specialises in serving undersized fish. Try the baby lobster and salmon fingerlings on a bed of tuna placenta.

✉ *21 Av Jorge Lopez*
☎ *37 258 879*
@ *dom@sombrero.com.ss*
▭ *V*

El Domingo This up-market bistro is popular with businessmen, diplomats and mid-level US intelligence operatives who come here to sample house specialities such as *Pollo y Pollo* (chicken stuffed with chicken) served on a bed of chicken. The atmosphere is described as 'sophisticated', meaning the restaurant is full of cigar smoke.

✉ *4 Av Jennifer Lopez*
☎ *37 695 179*
▭ *V DC*

Matsuwi This two-level Japanese restaurant offers a popular sushi bar using high-quality ingredients. The oohing and aahing from upstairs is generated by customers watching the trainee-teppanyaki chef who has just managed to slice into one of his fingers again.

Frederico's is an expensive eatery with a good selection of wine and food. It's a popular haunt for Cucaracha's *politicos* and so dress standards dictate a collar and bulletproof jacket. There's covered seating on the patio, with caged parakeets providing additional atmosphere (as well as emergency entrees should the kitchen run out of food).

✉ *132 Calle Santa Fiesta*
☎ *37 589 227*
@ *fred@eat.com.ss*
  patio

We Were Wrong. In our previous edition we stated that the Restaurant Capitolio's signature dish was aged beef, 'served with bearnaise sauce'. This dish is, in fact, 'served with bear sauce'.

FRENCH FLAIR!

Those wanting the ultimate dining experience in Cucaracha City need go no further than *Chez Noirel*, the showpiece of expat French gastronome Dominique Noirel. Born in northern France, Dominique started work as a kitchen hand at the prestigious Creton Fou restaurant where he quickly rose through the ranks and, by the age of just 17, found himself in charge of over twenty staff, many of them old enough to be his grandfather! (In fact, one was his grandfather, but Dominique had the old man sacked a few months later for insolence.)

With his short temper and lack of social skills it didn't take long for Dominique to realise he was ideally suited to becoming a chef and, by the age of 23, had opened one of the top restaurants in Paris. After a decade at the helm of *La Parouse,* Dominique realised that running a restaurant and married life do not mix and so, in 1997, he made the difficult decision and walked out on his wife, migrating to San Sombrèro where he now heads one of Cucaracha City's most expensive and exclusive eateries, *Chez Noirel*.

It's an exciting fusion of San Sombrèran food and French style, described by one recent critic as 'service with a sneer'.

☁☁ Mid-Range

✉ *908 Av Gloria Estoban*
☎ *37 259 745*
@ *am@cucaracha.com.ss*
▤ *V DC MC*

Ambrosia With its relaxed atmosphere and rough-hewn tables, Ambrosia is a great place to pop in for a rustic snack. Bunches of onions and peppers dangle from the ceiling, as do any diners foolish enough to attempt leaving without a tip.

✉ *885 Av Trini Lopez*
☎ *37 896 871*
@ *eatery@manolus.com.ss*
▤ *V*

Manolos This 24-hour eatery on the bustling pedestrian thoroughfare offers some of the city's best people-watching opportunities. (In fact, the Secret Police have a corner table permanently reserved.) The food is good and it's open seven days a week, closing only for religious holidays or after drive-by shootings.

We Were Wrong. In our last edition we mentioned that the Terraza Bar features an outdoor balcony where patrons are welcome to sit. They are, in fact, welcome to 'spit'.

✉ *1893 Calle San Rafael*
☎ *37 259 879*
@ *palacio@president.com.ss*
▤ *V MC*

El Café del Palacio Situated near the Presidential Palace, the slightly above average prices of this lively bistro are more than offset by its below average service. Be warned – the small bowl of pumpkin seeds served before your meal is not complimentary – it's entrée.

✉ *12 Calle Antonio Banderas*
☎ *37 821 567*
@ *café@cucaracha.com.ss*

Café Cucaracha Decorated throughout in traditional style (its walls covered with posters of heavyweight boxers and Pope John Paul II), this is an excellent mid-range choice. The waitstaff here all dress in authentic folkloric clothing (stained aprons) and your coffee is filtered through the traditional *chorreador* ('used dish cloth').

Traveller's Tip

Buffets are a popular way of eating out in Cucaracha City on a modest budget. Most buffets feature metal tongs – these are not for picking up food, they are used by staff to pinch diners caught overfilling their plates.

🕊 Budget

Ye Olde Cockerel Who would have thought? A taste of old England in downtown Cucracha. As its name suggests, the Cockerel is modelled on a British pub, with brick walls, heavy interior beams and a group of unemployed youths spoiling for a fight after a local soccer derby.

✉ *986 Blvd San Mustachio*
☎ *37 236 975*
@ *roar@lion.com.ss*
▤ *MC*

Jay Joe's A Tex Mex style eatery, heavy on the chillis and pimento dishes. Low prices mean you can be sure this place won't damage your wallet. The same cannot be said for your oesophagus.

✉ *78 Calle Emiliaz*
☎ *37 200 000*
@ *jay@joes.com.ss*
▤ *V MC*

Los Arracos Despite its status as a backpacker hang-out, this funky bakery has been internationally recognised – it was mentioned in a recent *World Health Organization* report. Most come for the excellent pastries, all of which are made by hand, which perhaps explains the occasional fingernail found within.

✉ *9 Calle San Felacio*
☎ *37 588 798*
@ *bake@funky.com.ss*

Naturalmente! Out front of this popular downtown establishment you'll find baskets filled with organic fruit and vegetables, while inside the walls are lined with herbal teas, health-food books and vitamin supplements. Odd really, as the place is in fact a cigar bar.

✉ *97 Av Gloria Estefan*
☎ *37 999 813*
@ *health@vitamin.com.ss*
▤ *V*

LOVE A LAUGH?
Many of Cucaracha City's bars and bistros play host to comedians. You'll need reasonably good San Sombrèran Spanish to get many of the jokes and, even then, it can be something of a challenge. One word of advice – be sure to laugh (or at least smile) as local comics don't take kindly to unresponsive crowds and they will often respond, in turn, with a version of 'audience participation' that may involve capsicum spray.

Attractions

Cucaracha City is divided into **three regions** of interest to tourists: the Old Town, the Harbour, and the hospital. Most visitors start by exploring the cobblestone streets of the historic **Old Town.** While this section of town is **traffic free**, few motorists adhere to this ban and visitors should be on the lookout for speeding vehicles in streets, alleys, pedestrian malls and even the **foyers** of some large city hotels.

Cucaracha City is also blessed with numerous **parks** and **grassy squares**. On sunny weekends dozens of *Cucas* (as residents of the capital call themselves) can be seen **jogging** through these, either to keep fit or simply to escape from gangs of serenading **mariachi** bands.

Numerous attempts are being made to inject culture into Cucaracha City and on just about any evening you can attend the opening of an art exhibition or – the following day – its closing. The **NATIONAL ACADEMY OF DRAMA** regularly presents local translations of **Shakespeare** plays and – given the speed of spoken San Sombrèran – you can actually enjoy all seven of his epic tragedies in the one evening.

The best place to see a concert in Cucaracha City is at the **TEATRO NACIONAL**, home of the **San Sombrèro Symphony Orchestra**. In an effort to reach the masses, the SSSO has done away with formalities such as tuxedoes or **tuning up**, and you can pick up a front row ticket to one of their recitals for less than $US10 (expect to pay a little more if you plan on sitting further away from the stage). **Classical** music audiences in San Sombrèro are enthusiastic but easily distracted and during some slower pieces it is not uncommon for a **Mexican Wave** to sweep across the auditorium.

THE PRESIDENTIAL PALACE is probably *the* feature attraction in Cucaracha City. The Palace was originally built by Spanish forces during the 16th century. This heavily **fortified** compound was famously captured during the *mardi gras* celebrations of 1756, when **rebel** troops stormed the building by forming a massive **conga** line. (In fact, the rebels of nearby Sierra Negra are still called the *Conganistas*.) These days the Palace is home to San Sombrèro's president but on **weekends** he opens it up to selected guests and visiting prostitutes. The most impressive part of the palace is the **Hall of Dignitaries** where numerous San Sombrèran presidents have been interred (many while still alive).

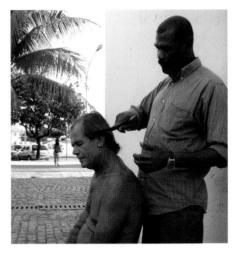

It's possible to get just about anything on the streets of Cucaracha City, including (clockwise from above): braiding, a shoe shine, a haircut, or even emergency chiropractic treatment.

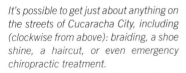

CATEDRAL SAN PEDRO APOSTOLO Built in 1867, this neoclassic structure was intended to be a faithful replica of Rome's St Peter's and, as a **match**, it's not far off, except for the fact that it is made out of **adobe**. Inside visitors are encouraged to purchase and light a votive candle or, during the wet season, votive mosquito coil. The cathedral features a **magnificent German-made organ** with over 6000 **pipes**. To enjoy its full majesty, come for high mass on Sunday or visit Tuesday night when the local Rick Wakeman Fan Club holds their meetings.

MUSEO NACIONAL San Sombrèro's largest and most impressive museum is housed in a magnificent Spanish colonial building to the west of the town **centre** and boasts an impressive collection of **artefacts**. The museum has dim lighting throughout, which not only helps preserve the delicate objects on display, but also masks the fact that most off them are reproductions.

PARQUE METROPOLITANO One of the largest green spaces in the city, this tree-filled square is popular with **locals** who come here to feed (and, in some cases, feed on) the pigeons. A statue of Alfonso Reyes, one of the city's most famous **campaigners for civil liberties**, stands in the centre, overlooking the square. Two closed-circuit cameras hidden in his eyes provide interior **ministry officials** with 24-hour surveillance of all activity.

AVENIDA OBRA is Cucaracha City's shortest street. It is appropriately named after its shortest **military leader**, General Pichito.

Visitors often remark on the way San Sombrèrans like to lounge in their doorways. In some cases they have no choice as they're serving home-detention sentences.

PLAZA MUNDO This small, shady square south of the Cathedral is popular with hawkers and **money changers** and can be a good place to get a shoe shine, unless you happen to be wearing sandals, in which case its best avoided.

PARQUE ZOOLOGICO Despite being extensively renovated in the 1990s, some **visitors** have reported that living conditions for many of the animals here are somewhat disturbing. Of particular concern, the **elephant hutch** and the **giraffe box**, as well as an alarming number of seals kept in 44 gallon drums. On a more positive note, several sections of the zoo have been improved, allowing many animals to live in **conditions** resembling their native habitats (denuded rainforest).

In an effort to cut costs the Cucaracha City Zoo has recently introduced a policy under which different species share the one cage. It has met with limited success.

Fast Fact. Visitors to the Cucaracha City Zoo are encouraged to feed the animals as, for many species, this is the only source of regular nourishment they are likely to get.

Helena Writes... **For the Eco-Traveller**
I have serious reservations about visiting zoos and will only do so if convinced that the animals exhibited there are well fed, properly housed, and free to leave at any time.

Another popular attraction is **MUNDO DE LAS SERPIENTES** (World of Serpents), which bills itself as Central America's first ever snake-petting zoo. There are various 'hands-on' displays and a **resident heptologist** is on stand-by to help identify your bite.

Note Most areas of Cucaracha City are safe after dark, although one should avoid the red-light district of San Felacio.

Cucaracha City

SOCCER CITY!

Cucaracha City's beloved *futbol* team, Atletico Huligano, is based at its stadium in the northern suburb of Guera. But on any Sunday or Wednesday you can get a taste of the excitement by watching clusters of fans decked out in their distinctive purple shirts and electronic security bracelets gathered in bars round any spare TV yelling 'Gooooooooooooooooooal!' In fact, the longest 'goooooooal!' ever recorded took place in the city back in 1974 – three hours, fifty two seconds. Everyone takes to the streets after a win and cars parade with team flags and the bodies of rival supporters hanging out the window.

IGLESIA SANTA MARIA This baroque house of worship was badly damaged by an **earthquake** in 1920 and an audacious ram-raid in 1983. The church has since been fully restored and attracts numerous **tourists** each day. A cassock-clad priest will permit visitors to follow him up the bell tower for a **breathtaking view** – initially of his underpants – and then the city itself.

CASTILLO MORRO Situated at the entrance to the harbour, this low-slung **castle** was responsible for protecting Cucaracha City from attack, a task it failed to achieve for more than 300 years due to the fact its **outer walls** were made of cork. Views from the main tower at sunset are spectacular. Unfortunately the **gates** shut at 3.30pm, so you'll have to take the security guard's word for it.

CEMETARIO Spread out over many acres of parkland, Cucaracha City's main **cemetery** boasts an impressive collection of mausoleums, **crypts**, family chapels and – somewhat disturbingly – its own food hall.

MUSEO CASA NATAL DE JOSE PERRI The birthplace of Cucaracha City's first mayor, his former home is now a museum and features various items of furniture and **personal effects**, as well as several great grandchildren in a specially designed display case. Whilst entrance to the museum is free, the **exit** involves passing through an extensive gift shop where visitors will be given the opportunity to purchase **commemorative** T-shirts, mugs and **spoon-ware**. Only after this will they be given the opportunity to leave.

BON VOYAGE!

Visitors to Cucaracha City's waterfront region will no doubt be struck by a large bronze plaque affixed to the end of the main dock. This marks the spot where the *Invincible*, a massive galleon loaded with gold and riches, set sail for Spain in 1802. Another plaque fixed to a channel marker about 50m away marks the spot where the *Invincible* sank, the victim of a poorly-aimed 21-gun salute.

Parque de Pueblo One of the city's largest and most popular green spaces, this park features a statue of **former rebel leader** Pedro Cira in a typical pose; cowering behind a palm tree. At the centre of the broad, open **square** is a replica of an 18th-century fountain that is itself a replica of a 15th-century replica built to replicate the original work, itself a replica. The **mosquitos** breeding in the stagnant water at its base are, however, real.

Museo de Armas Always popular, this well maintained museum features a macabre collection of leg irons, torture appliances and female depilatory devices that make for a truly gruesome **display**. Of particular interest is a **torture rack**, imported from Spain by zealous missionaries intent on stamping out paganism. Capable of stretching its unlucky **victim** by as much as 14cm, this is a copy; the **original** is currently on loan to the National Basketball Academy.

FASCINATING FACT

Cucaracha City's parks and squares have always played an important social role. It was here, during the late 17th century, that upper-class couples would come for their afternoon promenade or *passegio*, a delightful ritual that saw the men walking round in a clockwise direction, while the women circled in the opposite way. Historians consider this the first ever attempt at speed-dating.

LADY ON THE LOOKOUT

Cucaracha City's waterfront is dominated by the towering statue of *La Giradina*, set atop the harbour castle. The female figure gazing out over the water is said to represent Isla Giradina (1743–87), the wife of a former Spanish Governor. According to legend, she spent years staring at the horizon, waiting for her husband to return from his trade expedition to Spain. (In vain, it turned out, as he was in Mexico at the time, having married his mistress.)

The magnificent fountain of San Fernando was given to the people of Cucaracha City in 1642, a gift from the government of Spain. It was stolen two days later by local thieves and is yet to be replaced.

03 San Sombrèro
GUACOMALA PROVINCE

The Region

The most mountainous and often inaccessible area of the country, Guacomala Province, is San Sombrèro at its most **natural**. Here visitors can find steamy rainforests, waterfalls, **hot springs**, explosive geysers, exotic animals and – hopefully – their guide who will eventually return to lead them out of this extraordinary wilderness.

But, of course, it is Guacomala's volcanoes that draw so many people. The province boasts a staggering seven volcanoes, all of them **active**, and the sky is often thick with **choking sulphuric clouds**. Admittedly, much of this is generated by the Central Irzua copper **smelter**, but the region's volcanoes also produce an enormous amount of **ash** and smoke. In fact, living **next door** to a volcano can be the equivalent of smoking up to 15 packets of **cigarettes** per day. With this in mind, Guacomala's volcanoes are ranked Full Strength, Mild, Extra Mild and Menthol.

Corey Writes... For the Adventure Traveller

Guacomala Province is, of course, The place for volcanoing, the hot new sport of abseiling into the crater of an active volcano. Then there's 'vol-canoeing' (or 'red-water rafting'), in which you get to ride a lava flow down from the summit on board an asbestos-covered boat. What this ride lacks in speed it more than makes up for in danger. Hot stuff!

The main mountain range running through Guacomala is the *Cordilera Largato*. Its epic peaks and cavernous **valleys** are home to a wide variety of **exotic animals** and fascinating **indigenous tribes**. The animals can be extremely reclusive and difficult to spot – camouflaged clothing and a great deal of patience are generally required. The indigenous tribes, on the other hand, are **easier** to catch a glimpse of – most will be wearing brightly coloured Nike tops, plundered from a cargo plane crash site.

These Largato Ranges were, of course, the site of the tragic crash in 1974 when an Aero Sombrèro flight carrying members of the country's football team slammed into thick forest. Miraculously, eight people survived but, with searchers unable to locate them, these passengers were faced with an agonising decision. Eat the bodies of their dead companions, or eat the airline food. It was one of the most shocking acts of mass cannibalism every recorded.

In addition to volcanoes, the region experiences almost constant **seismic activity**, and much of its **colonial architecture** has been destroyed by earthquakes. In fact, the oldest intact building in Guacomala dates back to just 1966 – and that's a replica. So much a part of life are **earthquakes** in Guacomala that **school uniforms** now include a hard-hat.

Of course, Guacomala is not all mountains and volcanoes. Much of its **southern** section consists of low forest and farmland. Here one finds unique vegetation, such as the ancient **cork palm** (*Mycrocycas calocoma*), a botanical relic so rare that it is now considered a national treasure, after **decades** of being used as a popular source of kitchen flooring. This is a timeless country where **farmers** still plough their fields in the traditional way, using their wives.

When visiting active volcano regions look out for warnings that are posted daily and grade the likelihood of an imminent eruption:

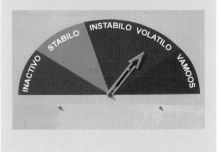

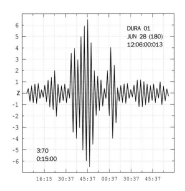

When Mount Abruzcon erupted in 1973 this seismograph was sent to various government agencies for official analysis. The Department of Seismology announced that it showed a tremor measuring 6.8. The Department of Intelligence announced that the volcano was lying.

Due to the large number of earthquake damaged buildings throughout Guacomala, restoration work is carried out selectively under the guiding principle 'if it ain't baroque – don't fix it'.

Fumarolé

The capital city of Guacomala Province is Fumarolé (pop. 75,000), an enchanting, if somewhat **sprawling centre**, perhaps most renowned for its wild, carefree *parradas*, unique year-end **carnivals** that tread a fine line between celebration and civil unrest.

The historic core of the city is the **Plaz Guerez**, named after the revolutionary hero Maximo Guerez. A **monument** records how he died (he was crushed to death by this monument). The square itself is dominated by an ornate, cast-iron **bandstand** that is still used as both a **concert** venue and a lightning conductor.

Adorning the skyline of central Fumarolé is the magnificent **Catedral de San Cristobel**. Built in 1803, this neo-Gothic edifice features columns and arches supporting **numerous spires** and turrets that soar towards the heavens. The cathedral is in remarkable condition, with only one small **spire**, on its left, missing, having collapsed in 1998 when a cell phone transmission dish was ill-advisedly attached.

Like so much of Guacomala Province, the city of Fumarolé has been **ravaged** by **earthquake damage**. Following a particularly bad 'quake in 1756, much of the city had to be rebuilt. Plans were drawn up by the then governor Eduard Carrero who designed the circular street layout, **central parklands** and residential sections, while his **wife** Isabella chose the colour scheme.

Visitors to Fumarolé are often struck by the unusual number of pink buildings found around its older streets. This colour scheme was actually achieved by mixing beef fat, blood, lime and turpentine – coincidentally the same ingredients used in many of the city's famous soups.

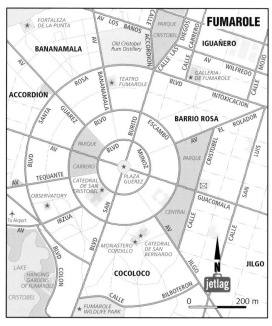

Visitors to Fumarolé may find themselves stopped in the street by a local and offered a 'free guitar' to take home. Check carefully, as this friendly stranger may well have packed the instrument full of drugs or – if he offers you a double bass – his relatives, in the hope of smuggling them out of the country.

History

The first people to inhabit the Guacomala region were the *metizo*, a tribe of **hunter-gatherers** who moved into the **southern slopes** around 2000 BC. An extremely advanced race, cave paintings suggest that the *metizo* may have been one of the first peoples in Central America to develop **writing**. Curiously, they never mastered the art of reading – so the impact of this breakthrough was somewhat limited.

Fumarolé's first female governor. A gifted leader, she centralised municipal control, established a civil service and introduced late-night shopping.

Archaeologists working in Guacomala Province recently uncovered this collection of rocks, believed to be one of the earliest public picnic areas ever constructed.

The first European to reach the province was a Spanish miner, Marcos Wilfredo, who arrived with his wife and **children** during the 1680s and began prospecting for **gold**. Armed with only a shovel, he managed to obtain a huge amount of this precious metal by beating the local Indian population over the **head** and stealing their jewellery. But with the onset of the **wet season**, followed by a string of native attacks, Marcos decided this was no place to stay with a family, so he fled to Cucaracha City, leaving his **wife** and children to fend for themselves.

Of course, local indigenous tribes did not take this colonial invasion well, and attacks on the town were common. In 1723, **heavily armed** members of the *ocha* tribe stormed Fumarolé's main garrison, taking its Spanish guards by **surprise** and forcing them to **retreat** to the garrison's castle. Rather than continue to attack, the *ocha* decided to simply cut off supplies and starve their **enemy** out. Sure enough, the plan worked and, weak from hunger, the Spanish surrendered some three hours later.

By the 19th century word of this bountiful, **mountainous district** had got out and it wasn't long before Quakers, Mennonites and various other religious groups started settling in the region, seeking a life of **peace and tranquillity**. Sadly, these rival **groups** soon began fighting over land with such unprecedented violence that one Amish community began manufacturing their own **automatic weapons** (using traditional methods, of course).

Like most of San Sombrèro, Fumarolé was swept up in the wider national push for **independence** from Spain. During the early 19th century one its most famous rebel leaders, Maximo Guerez, galvanised **resistance** by holding underground *incontradas* ('gatherings') where he would make long and rambling revolutionary speeches, before serving finger food. So **charismatic** was Guerez that, during one address to a room of over 500 followers, it was said you could hear a **pin** drop. A grenade pin, as it turned out, and over 14 members of the audience were killed.

FAMOUS FAMILY

Visit anywhere in Guacomala Province and you're bound to see the name Cristobel on buildings, streets, plazas and even a popular brand of lady's hosiery. One of the most successful businessmen to ever settle in the district, Evelino Cristobel came to the colony in 1704. A simple merchant, he built a modest home in Fumarolé and took a wife, unfortunately not his own, resulting in the newly arrived immigrant being almost run out of town. But Cristobel was a shrewd operator and soon amassed a considerable fortune through shares in the city's largest rum distillery. His offspring continued to accumulate wealth and, within a few generations, the Cristobel family dominated just about every aspect of city life. The family continued to play a dominate role in Guacomalan business life well into the 20th century, only to see their wealth and influence wiped out in the dot-com boom of the 1990s.

The remains of Fumarolé's magnificent Spanish Observatory. Built during the 17th century, it featured a massive sundial capable of accurately telling the time to within one minute. With the introduction of daylight savings in the 1970s an attempt was made to adjust this timepiece, by rotating it 12 degrees clockwise, resulting in the structure's partial collapse.

Where to Stay

Fumarolé offers a reasonably wide range of accommodation options. During quiet periods rates will often drop, along with general **standards of cleanliness**. Prices also tend to vary with location. The cheapest hotels are generally found round Barrio Rosa, although – as this is a **red-light district** – most rooms can only be rented for a maximum of three hours.

✑✑✑ Expensive

✉ 2 Blvd Munoz
☎ 85 875 154
@ alageria@hotel.com.ss
▭ V DC

Hotel Alageria One of Fumarolé's most luxurious places to stay, this handsome, art-filled hotel occupies a historic house right in the centre of town. Its 55 luxury rooms are full of antiques, from Mayan ceramics through to the beta video player.

✉ 102 Calle Carrero
☎ 85 987 485
@ mona@mansion.com.ss
▭ V

Hotel Monasterio This beautiful historic mansion used to be an old Benedictine monastery and is as much a museum as a hotel. Guests stay in converted prayer cells, surrounded by genuine religious art – baths are made out of converted baptismal fonts and even your wake-up calls come in the form of Gregorian chant.

✉ 6886 Blvd Colon
☎ 85 134 672
@ grande@sombrero.com.ss
▭ V MC DC

Melia Grande Set on almost two hectares, the Melia is a converted hacienda-style building surrounded by thick vegetation that buffers it from traffic noise. Unfortunately, the sound of nesting monkeys and raucous birds is almost as deafening. Expensive and highly rated, the Melia promises a lot but fails to quite deliver, perhaps explaining its recent entry in the *Misleading Small Luxury Hotels of the World* guide.

WARNING!
Many hotels in Guacomala have geo-thermal hot water systems. Extreme caution should be exercised when using the shower or bath as temperatures may fluctuate wildly without warning. Under no circumstances use the bidet.

☁☁ Mid-Range

Hotel Horizontes This faceless, two-storey hotel has 40 rooms, each with bathroom and phone. According to several reports, the hotel's ceiling fans are dangerously low and guests are generally advised to enter their rooms as if they were boarding a helicopter.

✉ *45 Calle San Luis*
☏ *85 521 482*
@ *horizontes@hotel.com.ss*
▤ *V MC DC*

Hotel del Bento Local resident Isobel Bento opens her immaculate home to guests. Devoutly religious, Isobel insists her guests say grace before meals and refrain from strong drink or language. Those staying more than two nights may find themselves facing a compulsory baptism.

✉ *40 Av Irzua*
☏ *85 698 963*
@ *hotel@bento.com.ss*

Casa Municipal Featuring soft lighting, large double beds and mirrors on the ceiling, this reasonably priced hotel is popular with both families and couples wishing to start one. The Municipal lacks a gymnasium but, as the hotel has no elevators, guests staying anywhere above the 10th floor should not find lack of exercise a problem.

✉ *5 Av Wilfredo*
☏ *85 117 842*
@ *casa@municipal.com.ss*
▤ *V*

Hotel Medio Not a bad option if you're prepared to do without luxuries such as TV and locks on the door, this basic hotel offers a range of reasonably priced rooms. Several even have a bath, although guests will be required to supply their own water.

✉ *859 Av Guarez*
☏ *85 996 739*
@ *medio@hotel.com.ss*
▤ *V MC DC*

Pensionne Rodriguez A good, basic hotel in downtown Fumarolé. Be warned though – the elevator and TVs, like most members of the Rodriguez family, do not work.

✉ *123 Calle Bibloteron*
☏ *85 972 672*
@ *rod@rodriguez.com.ss*

Traveller's Tip

When checking in, many San Sombrèran hotels will request a copy of your passport. Be warned that in some remote areas there are no photocopy machines and this task must be painstakingly undertaken by calligraphers or local artists – the process often taking several days to complete.

☁ Budget

✉ 9821 Calle San Luis
☎ 85 258 764
@ andina@hostal.com.ss
▤ DC

Hostal Andina A convivial, if somewhat threadbare, hostel with nearly 100 beds arranged in rooms all looking out onto a central toilet block. Rooms vary in size, as do the light fittings, doors, walls and floors, the entire establishment having been constructed from second-hand building materials.

✉ 7 Blvd Santa Rosa
☎ 85 975 267

The Centro Luxury Hotel is neither central, luxurious nor, for that matter, a hotel – it's a dormitory-style youth hostel with several dozen triple bunks packed into an unventilated cellar. Bookings not essential.

✉ 9821 Calle San Luis
☎ 85 552 645
@ los@aticos.com.ss
  rooftop terrace

Pencion Los Aticos Another good low-cost option, Los Aticos features a great rooftop terrace with panoramic views of the neighbouring office block's air-conditioning unit. Rooms have a rustic feel and the furniture is wicker. So too, unfortunately, is the bath.

Helena Writes...
For the Eco-Traveller
Landfill is a major problem in many developing communities, which is why I always make a habit of carrying my waste back home. Not only does this take the strain off local refuse collection services, unwrapping a rubbish bag months after you've returned is a wonderful way of re-capturing the magic and allure of a country like San Sombrèro.

Due to frequent earthquake activity, many hotel pools in Guacomala struggle to hold water and are often only suitable for toddlers or mosquito larvae.

Where to Eat

Guacomalans have their own distinct cuisine (by law, many local dishes are banned from being taken outside the province), and **typical fare** includes *pollo y rizo* (chicken with rice), *rizo y pollo* (rice with chicken) and simply *y*, a mash-like **substance** somewhere between chicken and rice. Salads can often be a disappointment, with just a wilted lettuce leaf and **slice of tomato**. Try asking for an *insalta deluxo*, which often features grated cucumber.

Numerous restaurants have opened up in Fumarolé over recent years, all of varying standards. As a general rule when **eating out**, look for a restaurant with a pleasant or **dramatic setting** – it should help take your mind off the poor service.

☕☕☕ Expensive

Comedor Guarida One of Fumarolé's more formal eateries (many of the waiters actually wear long pants), this elegant eatery is run by local chef Raymond Cuirez, a man renowned for what he can do with a goat (what he can't do with goat is clearly spelled out in his parole conditions).

✉ *52 Blvd Munoz*
☎ *85 224 558*
▤ *V MC DC*

El Capitana Dinner here is accompanied by a *caberet espectaculo*, in which performers re-enact great moments from Fumarolé's political history.

Warning! *Diners are advised against being part of any audience participation segments involving the years 1908–17.*

✉ *87 Av Guarez*
☎ *85 986 875*
@ *el@capitana.com.ss*
▤ *V*

La Casa de 17 One of the city's original eateries,La Casa is situated in a restored colonial building. Rustically themed, much of the brickwork is exposed, as are the waitresses who are forced to wear rather low-cut tops.

✉ *17 Calle Cristobel*
☎ *85 967 222*
@ *17@casa.com.ss*
▤ *V MC*

Nuova Ballarde Consistency is the key here – all meals are overcooked – and the bistro features a wide choice of meats, from pork and chicken to beef and armadillo. According to the menu, most of the dishes are 'cooked with red wine', a reference – it turns out – to the chef's inability to function without a drink.

✉ *90 Av El Rolador*
☎ *85 748 777*
@ *ballard@sombrero.com.ss*
▤ *V MC DC*

✑✑ Mid-Range

✉ *1 Blvd Santa Rosa*
☎ *85 679 323*
▤ *V MC DC*

El Rincon This popular bistro is generally described as 'down-to-earth' (it has no floor boards) and the service is so relaxed it borders on non-existent. If offered a table outside, be warned – there's no actual footpath and you will be on the road.

✉ *236 Av Bananamala*
☎ *85 998 758*

El Cochnito From the outside this squat and rather drab eatery looks like a seedy dive but it's worth remembering that looks can often be deceiving. Not, however, in this case, and the Cochnito is best avoided.

✉ *99 Calle Carrero*
☎ *85 774 875*
@ *mama@gusto.com.ss*
▤ *DC*

Mama Gusto This popular bistro features relatively authentic Italian cuisine, despite the inclusion of tropical fruit in just about every dish. Try the pineapple-infused lasagne or banana parmagiana.

✉ *88 Blvd San Burrito*
☎ *85 111 241*
@ *alamano@com.ss*

Don Alamano The food here tends to be a little on the heavy side (it takes three waiters to bring the pork banquet) but the atmosphere is relaxed and food reasonably priced. Views from the rooftop bar are extensive, if somewhat limited to a forest of TV antennas.

TIPS ON TIPPING
Unlike the bigger cities, leaving a gratuity is not automatically expected in Fumarolé and, the fact is, if your waiter has not provided good service then no tip is required, unless of course he is standing over you with a meat tenderising mallet, in which case a few coins followed by a hasty exit could be advisable.

◌ Budget

Villa Vieja While the food here is adequate, the setting is a little sparse, with just a few rough wooden tables in a threadbare room. During peak periods it may be necessary to bring your own chair.

✉ *976 Calle Las Diegos*
☏ *85 497 873*
@ *villa@vieja.com.ss*

La Congrito Rowdy, backpacker friendly bistro with walls decorated in a wide variety of colourful, peeling paint. Everything here tends to be covered in breadcrumbs, including the waiters, but you can eat well for very little.

✉ *8879 Calle Accordiòn*
☏ *85 234 981*

Casa Vivi Affiliated with Fumarolé University's Agricultural Science department, this good value restaurant offers a wide selection of discarded laboratory animals.

✉ *85 Av Guacomala*
☏ *85 657 934*

El Roca A $2 all-you-can-eat buffet might seem like great value but after a quick inspection of the food on offer you'll quickly realise that all you can eat here are the bread rolls. Look elsewhere.

✉ *66 Av Jilgo*
☏ *85 746 894*
@ *roca@san.com.ss*

FURTHER AFIELD
Throughout Guacomala Province you'll find *paladons*, private homes that have been turned into restaurants. If planning to eat at any of these establishments it's worth phoning ahead to give them time to shop and chain up the dogs.

Attractions

CATEDRAL DE SAN BERNARDO One of the first religious houses in the city, this cathedral was built in 1738. Sadly, it's **suffered** extensive damage over the years from earthquake, fire, **flood**, war and a brief period during the 1980s when it was used as a youth disco. Sporadic attempts at **restoration** have been made to the cathedral's interior but these have served only to detract from its **former grandeur**. The plastic pews, for example, look sorely out of place, as does the laminex altar. And the attempt to replace stolen statues with shop **mannequins**, whilst well intentioned, falls sadly short of the mark.

MONASTERO CORDILLO Set behind impressive walls to the east of the cathedral is the Cordillo Monastery. Built during the 17th century, this rambling **property** belongs to the Siestites, a **monastic order** founded – for tax purposes – by Brother Juan Siesto in 1645. Siesto believed firmly in the principle that work was a **distraction** from worship and so established a fraternity of monks dedicated to **rest** and relaxation. He set out each day's routine in the order's charter, beginning

with a silent sleep-in, followed by **morning prayers**, morning tea and then a series of rests, naps, snoozes and lengthy lie-downs. Visitors to the **monastery** can still observe Siestite monks as they go about their life of contemplation, guided by the principles of Poverty, Chastity and Obesity.

Fumarolé's historic 18th-century cinema was extensively damaged in 1920 by earthquake and then, again, in 1977 by the installation of Sensoround®.

Traveller's Tip

Those with an interest in botany should be wary of visiting the 'Hanging Gardens' of Fumarolé. Whilst there are some magnificent old trees, the sight of recently executed criminals swinging from their branches is not one for the faint-hearted. Nor is the sight of children using the bodies for a macabre local version of piñata.

Teatro Fumarolé Dating from 1863, this theatre is considered one of the finest in San Sombrèro. Performances are regularly held here and the **venue** hosts everything from **ballet** to mud wrestling. You can also visit the theatre outside of performance times but to do so you must either join an **organised tour** or **break in** through a window above the box office.

Galeria de Fumarolé Featuring an extensive collection of works from international and **local artists**, this museum includes a section dedicated to Martin Lanorte, the city's most prolific **nude artist**. Some of his best works are said to be so realistic that, when viewing them, the breasts appear to actually follow you round the room.

Fortaleza de la Punta This 17th century Spanish fort was designed to protect the city from native **attack**, and features massive walls, battlements, fortified keeps and even a **moat**. Completed in 1678, it was only during the **official** opening ceremony that its owners realised they'd forgot to include an **entrance**, and were forced to spend the next decade attempting to break in.

The Galleria de Fumarolé houses many great works of art, including Alvaro Domasquo's La Negriata ('the Black Virgin').

CINEMATIC STAR
Fumarolé-born Juan Jaruco (1952–) is one of the most prolific and respected film directors to emerge from Central America. He isn't frightened to abandon the constraints of narrative, plot, continuity and – in some cases – focus to present a deeply stylised vision of personal life. He wrote and directed some of San Sombrèro's most significant films, including *My Mother Myself* (1997), *Mother Love* (1999), *Mother Mother* (2002) and the enduring classic *Am I Not Good Enough For You Mother?* (2004). Juan still lives in Fumarolé with his mother.

Further Afield

While many visitors rarely venture outside of Fumarolé, there are numerous sights and attractions spread throughout Guacomala Province. Despite its steep hills, the region is heavily promoted as being perfect for **bicycle** tourism and many **couples** choose to attempt the scenic circuit road from Mantzarra to Piada. This trip usually takes around five hours, allowing for **arguments**. But, of course, it is the region's many **volcanoes** that draw so many people to Guacomala. Some of the most popular are:

VOLCAN IPOA, the province's most active volcano, dominates the **eastern skyline**. Its active crater often spews a plume of acrid smoke, as do the many buses that take tourists to its base.

VOLCAN TURRILO The summit of this volcano is accessible only by organised four-wheel-drive vehicle. Those planning an ascent of this **still-active crater** should pack warm clothes and be prepared to inhale fumes all day, as most of the guides smoke heavily.

VOLCAN CALDERON is an inactive volcano visited each day by tourist buses and hikers, as well as garbage trucks who make use of its cavernous **abyss** to dump refuse.

VOLCAN TENORIA last erupted in 2004. As a safety precaution all residents living nearby have since been evacuated and guided tour **ticket prices** reduced by 50%.

Often the only way to visit a volcano is as part of a guided tour. If you're looking for the intimacy you don't get in a big group, try Guacomala Adventures. Whilst this well-known local company often starts the day with large parties, its high accident rates generally ensure that, by lunchtime, you'll be down to just a few people.

Palacio Escambo One of the most beautifully preserved buildings in all of Guacomala, this **18th-century palace** served as governor Rauol Escambo's summer retreat. During August 1790 the colonial leader came here to beat the heat of Cucaracha City. Set high in the hills on an exposed slope, surrounded by shady trees and subject to cooling breezes as well as even the **occasional snowstorm**, Escambo spent several weeks here before his death from hypothermia.

Native to Guacomala province is the mountain llama. Its trusting nature and gentle personality make it an ideal barbecue meat.

El Arenal Parque Nacional One of the region's most popular national parks, El Arenal has suffered severe deforestation over the years, but most of its **picnic areas** are still lined with trees, albeit ones that have been felled and are awaiting removal. The park's vast lake is an excellent place to watch **waterfowl** such as Jabiru, Anhinga and Roseate Spoonbill being shot at by members of the local hunt club.

The Guacomala Bioparque For those unable to head deep into the forest themselves, this educational centre offers a fascinating insight into the **unique fauna** of the region. However, it should be noted that the Bioparque is sponsored by Pulpcom, one of San Sombrèro's largest **logging companies**, and therefore its message must be viewed with some caution, in particular the claim that old-growth forests represent a bio-hazard.

Visitors to the wildlife park in Fumarolé can get up close to the famous 'Kung Fu Monkeys'. Your admission price includes the cost of a rabies shot.

Helena Writes...
For the Eco-Traveller
If offered the chance to visit any of Guacomala's rainforests, remember to tread carefully. When visiting a fragile wilderness area I prefer to walk backwards, re-planting native grasses in my footprints.

POWERFUL PEPE

A humble looking home in the mountain hamlet of Pelaez is the birthplace of Guacomala's greatest athlete, Pieta 'Pepe' Mercurio. Born the son of indigenous farmers, Pepe developed his amazing strength by carrying water each day from a nearby well. After being selected to represent his country in weightlifting at the 1976 Montreal Olympics, he came close to winning gold, only missing out when judges ruled it illegal to lift weights using the head.

We Were Wrong. In our previous addition we said that 'the people of Mantzarra regularly enjoy cannabis'. This should have read that 'the people of Mantzarra regularly enjoy cannabilism'. Our apologies to any residents who may have been offended.

Casa Gavotte It was to this rambling country villa that local artist Gonzalo Gavotte came in the **summer** of 1960. Here he spent the summer with several nude models, busy – as he put it – 'exercising his muse'. As it turned out, Gavotte **failed** to produce a single finished work during this period but did manage to father 17 **children**, some of whom still live here and are happy to show visitors around.

Parada Caverns In 1983 a farmer in the mountain hamlet of Parada stumbled into a **hole**, and thus were discovered the *Carvernas de Parada* (Parada Caverns). The **limestone caves** contain a series of six chambers, five of which are open to the public (the sixth is still closed while rescue crews **continue** with their attempts to extricate the farmer).

Caverna San Munoz Another popular underground landmark, it was here in 1654 that **religious** leader Javier Munuz decided to make a retreat, entering this cave in the **hills** with just a Bible, a case of wine and his girlfriend. Munoz planned to spend 40 days here wrestling with his inner **demons** but was forced out after just two when his wife tracked him down.

Santo Rosa Parcque Nacional Stretching from the Riocas Valley up into the Pullerta Mountains, Santo Rosa National Park encompasses a 317 sq km preserve, the **bulk** of which is pristine, remote wilderness. Unfortunately, since the **damming** of the Riocas River, most of this is now under water but parts of it can be seen during **droughts** and in a series of photos displayed near the spillway.

These rapids are known to rafting enthusiasts as 'The Devil's Toilet', not so much for their treacherous currents as the E. coli *count of its water.*

Hooking Up!

San Sombrèro is fast being recognised as **a fishing paradise**, and Guacomala Province boasts numerous rivers and lakes where anglers can try their luck. It is also **possible** to fish some of the province's geysers, for those who prefer their catch already poached.

Gaspar (alligator gar), found in the south, these hard-fighting fish have a long narrow **snout** full of sharp teeth, as do many of the professional guides working in the area. Gaspar are a real challenge to land on **light tackle** but quite easy for anyone armed with a spear gun and torch.

Guapote (rainbow bass) are caught by casting plugs or small **kittens** from the shore. The best place to target this species is Lake Arunel where there is a fish farm with notoriously inadequate fences.

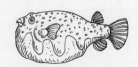

Sombrèran Snook This acrobatic species averages about 20 pounds and catching one is considered by many snook fishermen to be just about the most **exciting** experience imaginable. That said, the average snook fisherman spends much of his life **waist deep** in mud flicking maggots into stagnant pools, so this rapturous assessment must be **tempered** with that knowledge.

Jungle Trout Not native to San Sombrèro, trout were released into its rivers, along with cholera, by **Spanish settlers** sometime during the 18th century. Some have grown so **large** that they are now considered a threat to livestock and humans.

Professional fishing guides in Guacomala Province will not only clean and cook your catch, but – in many cases – eat it for you as well.

ALL ABOARD!

One of the great ways to explore central Guacomala is on board the *Tren a las Montas* (Train to the Mountains). The train, fully equipped with dining car, bar, guide and stewardess, leaves Torrida main station at 7.00am in the morning and reaches the 8500 foot summit of Mount Negro about seven hours later. The return trip back down the mountain takes less than half an hour, thanks to the locomotive's patently inadequate braking system.

Las Diegas

The peaceful mountain retreat of Las Diegas in Guacomala's west draws **thousands of visitors** each year. What used to be a difficult road trip and river **crossing** has now been made easier thanks to the construction of a $17 million **bridge**. The Ponte Nuevo crosses the Rio Tempbro just north of Las Diegas and has eliminated the long wait for the **ferry**. The only down side is that **snipers**, mainly disgruntled ex-ferry owners, are liable to take pot-shots at motorists using the structure. Under no account should you **stop** or get out of the vehicle.

Entering the historic settlement of Las Diegas one is struck by the **awesome power** of nature. Along this valley water and wind have carved out the **red sandstone** – freely available explosives have done the rest. If you're after picture-perfect photographs, pull off the road at the top of the **mountain pass**. A vendor based there sells **postcards** of what the valley looked like before the copper mine went in.

The 'Keep Las Diegas Beautiful' sign outside the town was taken down in 2003 after being deemed 'ironic'.

The drug trade in Guacomala Province is so highly developed that many larger dealers offer a free home-delivery service.

04 San Sombrèro
SAN ABANDONIO
PROVINCE

The Region

The north of San Sombrèro is often viewed as a dull, arid and **sparsely populated**, rocky semi-desert plateau, making its description in tourist promotional literature as the country's 'Riviera' somewhat misleading. However, the **intrepid traveller** will discover much to enjoy in this most 'authentic' of provinces.

Here one finds the highest percentage of **indigenous people** in San Sombrèro. Mainly descendants of the Huey tribe, these native groups still maintain traditional customs such as not paying **taxes**, and live as their ancestors did, without electricity or deodorant.

This is San Sombrèro's rural heartland. Where else can you drive across rolling **plains** and stumble upon a herd of **cattle** lined up in the holding pens of a stone abattoir? Or watch a colourfully dressed *gancho* (farmhand) branding his own children? On these **beef** farms nothing is wasted, not even the manure, which is dried and used for burning or to **flavour** the local cheese.

Sadly, the history of San Abandonio has been greatly dominated by warfare. So constant have battles, disputes and **border skirmishes** been, that the region's folkloric dress still features a **gun belt**. But despite their warlike reputation, the residents of San Abandonio are also a remarkably artistic people who produce a wide range of **hand-carved artefacts**. Admittedly, many of these are firearms and knives, but the workmanship cannot be questioned.

The central plateau area of San Abandonio is known as the *tierra caliente* (hot lands), an often remote, inhospitable **landscape** battered by strong, almost constant winds. Here **cattle** are the staple source of income and, so important are these beasts of burden, that in 1957 they were granted the 35-hour week.

A vendor sells fresh produce at San Abandonio's famous Mercado Narcotico.

San Sombrèro's fledging I.T. industry is based in San Abandonio. A lack of technical resources means that it is one of the few places in the world where computer chips are still carved by hand.

Nicotiño

For those willing to make the **effort**, Nicotiño is one of the most fascinating and vibrant of all San Sombrèran cities. Here people **dance on the streets** and the fact that many live on them too in no way **detracts** from the ebullient charm of this provincial city.

Whilst urban **sprawl** and industrial development have taken their toll on Nicotiño's scenic beauty, the city still ranks as one of San Sombrèro's most **picturesque**, and in recent years local **authorities** have worked hard to improve its tourism infrastructure, reflected in a **new airport**, modern hotels and moves to introduce street drainage.

A lack of rain, top-soil and restrictions on logging have all contributed to Nicotiño's distinctive 'scorched earth' appearance.

The centre of Nicotiño is marked by its expansive Parque Central. This broad **plaza** is delightfully shady (it's surrounded on all sides by high-rise office blocks) and has always been considered the **cultural heart** of the city, despite the fact that Monday to Friday it is used as a **car park**.

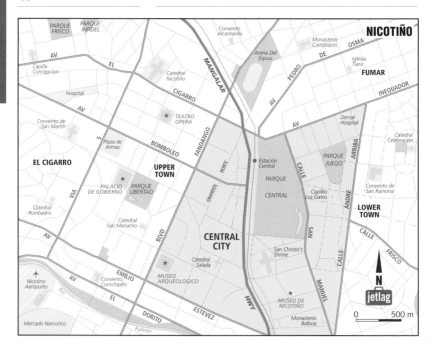

The city centre itself is divided into the **Lower and Upper Towns**. The working class Lower Town has always had something of a seedy side, attracting thieves, **beggars** and, of course, members of the city's **oldest profession**, taxi drivers. Caution should be taken when visiting this area.

During the 1990s Nicotiño developed an unfortunate **reputation** as a city plagued by petty crime and violence. The problem was clearly linked to police numbers – there were too many – and moves to **decommission** excess officers have subsequently been implemented.

SECURITY TIP

Visitors should exercise common sense and avoid areas of obvious danger such as darkened streets or public schools. For those driving, remember to never leave anything in plain view in an unguarded car. This includes personal belongings, stereo, tyres, windscreen wipers, registration plates and easily unbolted sections of the engine.

Music plays a major part in Nicotiñoan life and everywhere you'll see and hear traditionally dressed *rhonero* performers. This ancient ballad tradition resembles Portuguese *fado* with lengthy, melancholic songs telling of lost love and grief. Passers-by offer tips in the form of loose change or anti-depressants.

History

The earliest evidence of human **occupation** in San Abandonio comes in the form of a series of hollowed-out, **upright stone blocks** (left), or 'menhirs', dotted across the treeless central plains at intervals of about a mile. Dating from the Neolithic period (4000–2400 BC), these structures were originally thought to have religious or **astronomical significance**, however, scientists now believe them to represent one of the largest continuous networks of public **urinals** ever erected.

The first group of people to permanently **settle** in the region were the Ux'Uachuan who survived by collecting seeds and fruits. Facing opposition from **neighbouring tribes**, by around 3000 BC the Ux'Uachuan developed into hunters – each day the men would go out and spear plants.

The Metizo people (300–1500 AD) lived in simple **thatched huts** (right), built on a mound of earth to avoid spring floods. When a family member died, burial took place right there in the living room, giving the dwelling immediate **sacred power**, although somewhat diminishing its re-sale value.

ANYONE FOR JUEGO?

The recreation most favoured by the Metizo was a ball game (*juego de corro*) in which players had to keep a hard rubber ball airborne using any part of their body other than their hands, head or feet. Contests were taken very seriously and poorly performing players could expect to become human sacrifices or, worse, lose their sponsorship deals.

Spanish Conquest

The Metizo were, in general, a peaceful race but when threatened or woken early they could turn into fearsome **warriors**. However, they were no match for Spanish forces who arrived in 1523, under the command of Hernan Corvez. The battle was brief but brutal. Corvez and his troops had **horses**, **guns and swords**. The Metizo had brightly painted **masks**. The Spanish won without losing a single man, their only injury being Corvez's second-in-command who sprained his ankle during an overly energetic victory dance.

During the 18th century sugar and rubber became the **staple crops** of the region and thousands of slaves were brought over from Africa to work the plantations. While most of the **sugar** was exported to Europe, Spanish troops based in San Abandonio came up with an ingenious use for local rubber, using it to make cannonballs. This practice was only abandoned in 1595 when **several artillery rounds** bounced back on soldiers, wiping out half a battalion.

FASCINATING FACT

In 1863 the mongoose was introduced to catch snakes in the cane fields. This plan backfired soon after when the mongoose and the snakes teamed up, launching a string of concerted attacks on sugar cane workers.

Independence

As in other parts of San Sombrèro, the push for independence from colonial rule gathered pace over many **generations**. By the early 19th century the people of San Abandonio were openly calling for **liberty and equality**. Instead they got smallpox and continued brutal **repression**. But eventually people power won out and, in 1879, the Spanish were forced to flee, leaving San Abandonio under the control of one-time freedom fighter turned **military strongman** General Avalres. Alvares was a man of strict morals and ordered that all 'undesirables' – homosexuals, criminals and communists – be driven out of the province. This **order** had to be revoked when Avalres realised it would have halved his family.

The Metizo's astronomical observations and calculations were uncannily accurate. Using these simple stone structures, they could pinpoint eclipses and cycles of Venus hundreds of years ahead. Curiously, they struggled to ever determine which was bin night.

GABRIEL GOMEZ
THE FATHER OF SAN ABANDONIO INDEPENDENCE

Born in Nicotiño in 1836, Gomez was a deep **political thinker** who wrote books and extensive articles denouncing Spanish sovereignty, along with **anti-government tracts**, satirical stories and even nationalistic poetry.

His passion for the written word almost had him killed when, in 1862, he received a tip-off that a bomb had been planted in his house yet insisted on staying in the study to compose a **ballad** denouncing state-sponsored repression.

Gomez, circa 1864.

In 1865 Gomez was arrested by Spanish authorities and **exiled** to the island of Cuvarecha, off San Sombrèro's east coast, where he spent many years producing lengthy **pro-independence** treatises.

In 1872 Gomez decided to return, chartering a small **boat** into which he loaded his last seven year's writings. Tragically, the boat immediately sank beneath the voluminous **weight** and Gomez only made it to San Sombrèro's mainland by clinging to one of his more **buoyant** short stories.

On the evening of 23 June 1873 he finally returned home to Nicotiño where he wasted no time in calling a meeting of local freedom fighters, giving each of them a copy of his **epic revolutionary tome** *La Patria Libre* to read. Six weeks later no-one had made it past chapter three and it was decided that the group look to more **immediate methods** of civil insurgency. Most favoured an armed attack on Spanish **troops** based at the city barracks but Gomez preferred **mailing** them a series of strongly worded essays. In the end a compromise was reached – a lengthy **letter bomb** was sent – and the campaign for independence was underway.

Denim is considered so fashionable that many Nicotiño homeowners use designer jeans as blinds.

KEEPING THE BEAT

In San Abandonio you might be lucky enough to witness the *colombria*, an exuberant men's dance performed blindfolded with machetes, its complex rhythms clapped out by the dance leader with his one remaining hand. Or hear the *tubon* (below), a native woodwind instrument that produces a sound likened to that of water going down a narrow plug-hole.

Nicotiño Cathedral's famous jewel-encrusted statue of Christ the Redeemer was completed on 5 September 1706 and stolen the next day.

Where to Stay

Nicotiño has a **reasonable range** of accommodation options, but little that is particularly appealing at the budget end. In fact, **seasoned backpackers** recommend getting **arrested**, as a police holding cell is considered a preferable alternative to any of the city's hostels.

Traveller's Tip

Faulty hotel electric hot water units can make taking a shower somewhat hazardous as shocks are not uncommon. In fact, criminals sentenced to death in San Sombrèro will often be sentenced to *ducha caliente*, literally, the shower cubicle.

☁☁☁ Expensive

✉ *52 Blvd Fandango*
☎ *23 872 659*
@ *ami@sombrero.com.ss*
🛏 *V*

Hotel Americano One of Nicotiño's oldest luxury hotels, the service here is both impeccable and formal – even the pick-pockets hanging round the hotel lobby wear white gloves. Rooms are all large and have an air of colonial grandeur, although this might just be the brand of carpet deodoriser they use.

✉ *223 Av Bombeleo*
☎ *23 658 141*
@ *madi@grande.com.ss*
🛏 *V MC*
   beauty salon

Madisson Grande One of the largest up-market hotels in Nicotiño, the newly-renovated Madisson even boasts a floor exclusively for women (with a beauty salon and sauna!) and one for men (with peep holes in the floor providing a full view of the aforementioned sauna).

✉ *157 Calle San Manuel*
☎ *23 877 029*
@ *palace@chichen.com.ss*
🛏 *MC*

The Chichugan Palace is a pyramid-shaped limestone hotel built in the style of a traditional Mayan temple. They've certainly captured the feel of these ancient edifices – the place is cavernous, dank and smells as if someone has been buried in the lobby. All rooms feature thatched roofs and are decorated with ancient carvings depicting various gods and what they would do in the event of a fire.

Tina Writes... For the Cautious Traveller

When staying in a strange hotel room always be on the lookout for faulty locks on the door, spiked drinks in the mini bar, hidden cameras above the shower recess and drug dealers posing as innocent members of staff. On no account should you allow yourself to fall asleep.

☕☕ Mid-Range

Pencion Moderno Relaxed, friendly and cheap, the Moderno has been a popular hotel for years. Its English-speaking owner, Jose, was born in Nicotiño and remains an amiable host to travellers (a little too amiable, according to some female guests, who recommend declining any of his repeated offers to 'turn down the sheets').

✉ *98 Av El Cigarro*
☎ *23 007 833*
@ *playa@palace.com.ss*
▤ *V MC*

El Gran Pavo One of the city's best mid-range accommodation options, the Gran Pavo offers free airport transfers but, as their courtesy bus only makes the trip once a month, these are of limited value.

✉ *25 Calle Frisco*
☎ *23 871 578*
@ *gran@pavo.com.ss*
▤ *V MC*

Hostal Nicotiño Good basic rooms make up for a lack of service here. Reception does not provide wake-up calls but, as the chef is constantly burning the breakfast, you're just as likely to be woken by the sound of a smoke alarm.

✉ *455 Av Inequador*
☎ *23 801 359*
▤ *DC*

Ask the duty manager about discounts and upgrades; you won't get any but it's a good opportunity to learn some San Sombrèran expletives.

Hostal del Paseo A little out of town but with plenty of features including TV, internet, mini bar and hot tub. Unfortunately, these are all in the manager's room and off-limits to guests.

✉ *1003 Av Pedro de Osma*
☎ *23 533 668*
@ *gran@pavo.com.ss*
▤ *V*

Many hotels in Nicotiño offer a free hotel shuttle bus service.

🍽 Budget

✉ *255 Av Emilio Estevez*
☎ *23 998 351*
@ *artes@hostal.com.ss*

Hostal de las Artes Conveniently located in the city centre, this well-run hostel is popular with backpackers. Rooms are small and could do with a few extra creature comforts (such as mattresses) and the ceilings are a little low, but this is not a major issue unless you plan on standing upright during your stay.

✉ *598 Av El Cigarro*
☎ *23 112 094*
▤ *MC*

La Posada Nicotiño An always popular option, the Posada offers a dozen clean and comfortable rooms. Showers here are cold water only, but this is not a problem as none of them actually work.

✉ *4 Via 5*
☎ *23 987 016*
@ *lunas@smoko.com.ss*

Hostel Lunas This popular backpacker destination made headlines some years back when a fire broke out in an upstairs dormitory. A smoke alarm in the main office alerted the manager who wasted no time in evacuating the building. Unfortunately, he did so without warning any of the hostel's guests, many of whom were seriously injured. Their loss is your gain with smoke-damaged rooms available for a 30% discount.

✉ *9 Calle André Arriba*
☎ *23 998 015*
@ *budget@parti.com.ss*
▤ *V MC DC*

Parti! Probably the hippest joint in town, this is where budget travellers meet up to exchange information and – often unwittingly – gastric pathogens. Shared bathrooms are standard, as are – on most weekends – shared beds.

Traveller's Tip

Even cheaper hotels in Nicotiño will often have a pool, although guests should be warned – many of these may be somewhat limited both in terms of size and chlorine levels.

Where to Eat

The *Grandos Norte*, situated in the heart of Nicotiño, is the name for a two-block pedestrianised strip of restaurants and cafés with **sidewalk tables**. For some good up-market dining options, the area around Via 5 is where local business and political leaders come to **wine**, dine and occasionally be shot at by disgruntled citizens. For those on a budget, try Av Pedro de Osma, a street generally known as 'Little Italy' for its scores of **pizzerias** and high incidence of motor vehicle accidents.

✆✆✆ Expensive

Luis y Marie Run by a husband and wife team, this chic modern restaurant is popular with business travellers and tourists alike. Out back of the main dining room is an open kitchen where chef Luis can be seen terrorising his junior cooking staff. At evening's end his wife Marie will often take a chair and join diners to outline in detail her most recent medical procedures.

✉ *41 Av El Dorito*
☎ *23 514 975*
@ *luis@marie.com.ss*
🍴 *V MC*

Los Pueplos boasts a menu offering the 'magical' cuisines of pre-Columbian San Sombrèro. Bananas, corn and palm leaves feature heavily, all served in a typical indigenous style (on the floor). Classic San Sombrèran dishes are accompanied by drinks such as *barfo*, a fermented guava juice more commonly used as a bathroom disinfectant.

✉ *23 Blvd Fandango*
☎ *23 232 232*
@ *magical@pueplos.com.ss*
🍴 *V MC*

Adobe Z'ec Another native-themed eatery, this magnificent restaurant is actually set in the grounds of an adobe pyramid built by the original inhabitants of Nicotiño. Banquets are popular here, and the pork stuffed with orange is a delight for everyone (with the obvious exception of the pig). The best tables have views out over the ancient burial ground said to contain the remains of several 17th-century warriors as well as a recent diner who tried stealing a linen napkin.

✉ *221 Calle San Manuel*
☎ *23 971 855*
@ *native@adobe.com.ss*
🍴 *V MC DC*

El Verde Popular with businessmen and local politicians, you can dine outdoors or behind bulletproof glass and, for those worried about poisoning attempts, El Verde offers an on-site professional food-taster. This classic old-style café is staffed by waitresses in folkloric red-and-white *voluma* (lingerie). For an authentically local touch, all desserts are served with a dusting of icing sugar or cocaine.

✉ *12 Av Inequador*
☎ *23 007 458*
@ *verde@eat.com.ss*
🍴 *MC*

Traveller's Tip 👍

Several restaurants in Nicotiño offer home delivery but this service is advised against due to the fact that their frequently underpaid drivers will rarely resist the temptation to 'sample' some of your food order en route.

🍂🍂 Mid-Range

☒ *128 Mangalar Hwy*
☎ *23 985 394*
@ *leftbank@bakery.com.ss*
▤ *V MC*

The Left Bank Bakery A local institution, this lavish French-style establishment is run by expatriate Emile Pernot who boasts he can fill croissants with anything you like: ham, cheese, guacamole, sardines, mashed potato or even rack of lamb. In fact, it's the only bakery in the world to offer a croissant called the 'Quarter Pounder'.

☒ *32 Grandos Norte*
☎ *23 007 698*
@ *rustico@com.ss*
▤ *V*

Antico Rustico Diners should look out for a pretty yellow colonial house amidst the hustle and bustle of downtown Nicotiño. Inside you'll find deep red walls, black-and-white tile floors and large mirrors. A perfect place for lunch or dinner, but unfortunately it's an interior design showroom. The restaurant is next door, in a poorly ventilated shed.

☒ *589 Av Pedro de Osma*
☎ *23 041 842*
@ *italy@trattoria.com.ss*
▤ *V MC DC*

La Trattoria Autentica Despite being San Sombrèran-born, local chef Pasquale Luez has gone to great lengths to set up this Italian-style bistro. Some of this effort has been misguided (for example, photos of the Eiffel Tower above each table) but the food is generally good. Amongst the many homemade pastas are several stuffed versions, such as the anglotti with three meats: rabbit, pork and rabbit.

Traveller's Tip 👍

Some restaurants in Nicotiño can be a little difficult to spot from the street because they have been combined with bookshops, galleries, up-market car dealers or internet cafés. In fact, if anything looks like a restaurant from the outside then chances are it's not. (Right) A typical Nicotiño restaurant.

Restaurante Morada Despite its inland location and obvious lack of refrigeration facilities, this restaurant specialises in seafood. Most of the dishes come smothered in aromatic herbs, although this does little to mask the smell of week-old prawns (*camarones pongo*). Often busy on weekends, you can dine indoors but most prefer to eat in the courtyard where the mosquitoes are marginally less irritating than the Morada's resident folk combo.

✉ *12 Blvd Fandango*
☎ *23 985 996*
@ *seafood@morada.com.ss*

Visitors to Morada have always long enjoyed the antics of 'Pancho' the resident donkey who would entertain diners by guzzling beer. Sadly, Pancho has recently passed away but his liver remains on display.

San Abandonio's beautiful yellow-crested parrot is often known by its common name asando de dia (roast of the day).

A street food vendor, or colesterolla, *whips up a variety of deep-fried delicacies.*

⊘ Budget

Fast food joints abound in Nicotiño. **Pollo Frito** is the city's KFC clone, although for a more local touch there's also a KFT (Kentucky Fried Toucan). Another **low-cost** option is the Munchos chain. An interesting concept in lunchtime eating, diners here serve themselves from a cental **buffet** and are then charged per mouthful. Also popular are Nicotiño's many *rosticerias*, or roast chicken shops, serving **tasty meals** with beer in a lively atmosphere. The only downside is that these establishments tend to get pretty **noisy**, due both to the patrons and the chickens (which are killed to order).

✉ *2 Grandos Norte*
☏ *23 852 064*

El Establo This atmospheric old drinking den serves fine draft beer and tapas. Che Guevara himself once stopped for a drink here and – according to legend – his motorbike was stolen, prompting the revolutionary leader for the first time ever to openly curse the working class.

✉ *12 Calle Frisco*
☏ *23 174 066*

Café Amigo One of Nicotiño's busiest backpacker eateries, this bustling bistro was temporarily closed down in 2004 when a city health and sanitation inspector found something disturbing in the kitchen's freezer – one of his former colleagues. Following a major spring clean, Café Amigo is now open again and back to its slapdash best.

ROOM SERVICE
Throughout Nicotiño you will find numerous private homes, or *casiendas*, that operate as restaurants. These offer an excellent informal dining alternative and give a real taste of family life, although beware – you may be asked to help the children with their homework.

Attractions

Despite the noise, grime, crime and inappropriate development, there is much to see and **enjoy** in Nicotiño. Visitors with just a day or two to spare might like to check out the city's numerous museums and **historic buildings**, before catching a cultural show. Those with a week or more scheduled here might speak to their **travel agent** about a new itinerary.

PLAZA DE ARMAS The original centre of the city, this square is essentially a modern reconstruction. The disastrous 1743 **earthquake** levelled most of the original buildings here. Those that remained fell victim to the 1980s boom in low-cost **apartment block** construction.

TEATRO REGIONAL is Nicotiño's spectacular opera house. It was built during the 1850s and has, over the years, featured many great touring artists. In the basement you can see a small but fascinating collection of **theatrical artefacts**, including Enrico Caruso's favourite **gold watch**, kindly donated to the museum by the stagehand who stole it.

MUSEO ARQUEOLOGICO Despite boasting one of the most impressive collections of historical artefacts in San Sombrèro, this museum is perhaps most famous for its pre-Columbian **erotic ceramics** and carvings. Located outdoors in a courtyard garden setting, these works were produced by the local **indigenous** X'uata tribes-people around 600 BC. The X'uata depicted sex in a range of fascinating, if somewhat explicit ways, and the statues on display leave little to the imagination! (As do the local university students who often use **shady** sections of the courtyard for afternoon trysts.)

So many of the nation's soccer players have been convicted of match rigging that prison games regularly attract large crowds.

Palacio de Gobierno The former headquarters of colonial government in Nicotiño (left), this **ornate palace** was built during the dictatorial rule of General Jorge Oprez. Visits are by guided tour and are **free**, although a **tip** to your guide is a good idea, especially if he knows which hotel you are staying at. The entrance hall is dominated by an optimistic **mural** depicting Nicotiño's history of peace and freedom. Sadly, much of it has been badly damaged by gunfire.

Museo de Nicotiño Though small, this museum is worth a quick visit. It boasts over 7000 pieces, unfortunately, they're all from the one **exhibit**, a magnificent pre-Mayan ceramic **bowl** dropped by a drunk curator.

Museum of Sugar This impressive building illustrates just about every stage of the sugar production **process**, from planting of the canes through to tooth decay.

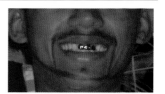

HORSING AROUND!

For many visitors to Nicotiño, the **must-see attraction** is the city's famous Dancing Horses. Each day crowds flock to the *Arena Del Caballo* to see these noble beasts perform intricately **choreographed sequences**, guided by just a few words and a great deal of whipping. The Dancing Horses of Nicotiño are trained to perform a series of specific and technically challenging moves such as:

Spanish Walk — horse lifts each front leg and throws it forward
Courbette — horse stands on hind legs and then jumps forward
Bulula — horse taps front hooves to a Hollywood showtune
Bolta — horse jumps a fence and heads towards Mexico

Each routine is tightly choreographed to classical music although, in an effort to perhaps move with the times, some shows now feature contemporary **soundtracks**. Of course, the sight of recreationally drug-affected horses swaying to a techno beat lacks the majesty of more traditional performances. They do, however, go until 4am.

Corey Writes...
For the Adventure Traveller

Don't even think about visiting Nicotiño without trying the hot new craze of 'draining'. Dressed in protective gear and helmet you slide head-first through the city's extensive underground sewerage system, before emerging at high speed from a storm water pipe on the outskirts of town, without having seen or heard a thing. I tell you what, it's an absolute blast, especially after heavy rain.

San Sombrèrans are justifiably proud of their artistic heritage and, at museums such as this one in Nicotiño, objects of cultural significance are on display. Sadly, many of these objects are also on sale, a reminder of the country's urgent need for hard currency.

Holy Town

Known as the 'City of Churches', Nicotiño has more cathedrals, chapels, **convents** and monasteries than just about anywhere else in San Sombrèro. In fact, there are said to be 132 individual houses of **worship** here (133 if you count the casino) and no visit would be complete without touring some of the more significant buildings.

CONVENTO DE SAN MARTIN Probably the most spectacular of Nicotiño's colonial-era churches, the Convent of Saint Martin attracts many tourists because of its **extensive catacombs**. Built during the 16th century, these tombs are said to hold almost 75,000 bodies, along with the parish priest's personal **wine collection**. A resident **caretaker** offers guided tours; his knowledge of history is excellent but sense of direction sadly lacking, so be sure to allow plenty of time.

CONVENTO DE SANTA RAMONA In stark contrast to the grandeur of many of Nicotiño's religious buildings, this humble convent is small and **plainly decorated**. Still operating today, it is home to the Ursulites, the first order of catholic nuns to wear **high-heeled shoes**, in the belief that this form of **footwear** would take them closer to heaven.

SAN EUFEMIO'S SHRINE This elegant chapel in a busy **downtown** street is dedicated to Nicotiño's much loved patron saint Eufemio de los Esperos. Numerous miracles have been attributed to St Eufemio and, despite not yet having been officially **canonised** by the **Catholic Church**, he is well on the way, having been featured in a made-for-TV bio-pic.

PAPAL VISIT

For Nicotiño's many Catholics, 1984 was a special year as Pope John Paul II paid a visit to their city. In preparation for the event, a public holiday was declared, meaning not a single member of the organising committee showed up for the official welcome. Things got even worse when the 'Popemobile' was wheel-clamped during a youth mass.

WARNING

Nicotiño's many parks are filled with loveable monkeys who swing from the trees and cheekily attempt to steal food from unwitting visitors. However, a disturbing recent trend has seen several groups of these primates actually begin to steal cameras and other valuables such as credit cards. Their modus operandi involves one member creating a distraction by 'playing dead' (see right) while several accomplices move in and remove the victim's wallet. Take care.

An ice-cream 'van' brings frozen treats to the children of San Abandonio, luring them with its distinctive 'eew-aww' chimes.

Further Afield

For many visitors to the province of San Abandonio, the area to the north-east of Nicotiño might seem to hold little **obvious** attraction. A massive region of **arid salt plains** interspersed by scrubby hills, these lands were actually handed back to their traditional indigenous owners in the mid-20th century, only for the **owners** to refuse the offer. But for those willing to make the **effort**, a trip into the hinterland has much to offer.

The picturesque township of **TINEÀ** lies about two hours east on the main inland highway. This sleepy town is well worth a visit although on no account should you stop or get out of your car. Once a **major sugar producing centre**, the abolition of legal **slavery** in the 1980s hit the town hard, forcing the people to fall back on their original staples of ambushing passing vehicles, and tourism.

Another provincial centre of interest is **FUNGALÉ**, a lively **market town** at the base of the Mangalar foothills. Fungale comes to life each year in September when the Harvest Festival is celebrated, to give thanks for the **fertility** of the earth. A young peasant girl is chosen to play the part of the maize god; she dresses up in bright clothes and sprays on-lookers with **chemical** fertiliser.

LA RUTA is another fascinating rural centre in the far west of San Abandonio. One of the most **popular** places to stay in La Ruta is at the Casona Ruta, a 18th-century **colonial hacienda** that now functions as an inn. The rustic architecture of this former farmhouse,

with rough **stone walls** and pitched beam roof, would be delightful if they would just clean up the manure and install some air-conditioning. **Photos** of the owners (left) provide a **homely** touch, not to mention a chilling reminder of the **skin damage** sun exposure can wreak.

*San Abandonio's arid regions receive very little rainfall and species such this cactus pine (*balsa dessicatus*) survive on the perspiration of visiting tourists.*

HOLY INHABITANTS

La Ruta is probably best known as being a centre for the **Hubnaker**, a fundamentalist religious sect founded during the 16th century by Dutchman Jan Hoergel. The Hubnakers fled Europe during the 1580s following a dispute with the Quakers over who first came up with the idea of having a beard without a moustache. Visitors to La Ruta will frequently come across Hubnaker communities, working the fields in their distinctive bib-and-tucker overalls and straw Stetsons (these are the women; Hubnaker men wear long black dresses). Feel free to  say hello but don't be surprised if they don't respond – the Hubnakers speak a form of Dutch-Spanish that is virtually unintelligible even to them. And remember – no photos! The Hubnakers believe photography to be the work of the Devil and have been known to attempt exorcisms on anyone holding a digital camera.

Wine Country

Anyone interested in San Sombrèran wine should definitely allow **time** for a visit to the Ayabca region of central San Abandonio. Here you'll find dozens of **artisanal wineries** (or *bodegas*) where wine is still made in the traditional manner – without any obvious form of **sterilisation**. These home-based operations produce a wide range of varieties, much of which are generally considered 'table wines' (used to strip **varnish** from furniture) but there are  also some unique local offerings such as *pisca*, a **shiraz-style** red so astringent that in some areas it is used by dentists as an oral anaesthetic. Attempts at substituting **coconuts** for grapes have met with some success, producing a sweet varietal that can be drunk as a dessert wine or used to **poison** wasps. Several of the region's *bodegas* welcome visitors; however, those contemplating a **wine tasting** should remember that it is not only polite, but compulsory, to **purchase** a few bottles after touring. Visitors attempting to leave without doing so may find themselves **fermenting** along with the wine.

05 San Sombrèro
LAMBARDA PROVINCE

Lambarda Province

The exotic **eastern** province of Lambarda is home to some of San Sombrèro's most **popular beaches** and resort towns. For all the excesses of inappropriate development and resulting **environmental damage**, this stretch of coast remains breathtakingly beautiful, especially when viewed at night. Chic, sexy, **cosmopolitan** and often expensive, the Lambarda coast is where San Sombrèro's **beautiful** people come to sip $US12 cocktails served by drink waiters who wouldn't earn that much in a year.

But don't make the mistake of viewing the province as purely a 'party zone' with little to offer other than sun-drenched **hedonism**. Inland you'll find some **excellent** Mayan ruins and – despite the fact that many have been turned into **casinos** – a visit is well worthwhile. Historically, Lambarda is also home to some beautifully preserved colonial towns such as Banderas, with its cobbled streets and quaint **white-walled**, terracotta-roofed government detention centre. And culturally, there are countless historic buildings, fine **art galleries** and Madame Tussaud's only **Brazilian Wax museum**.

FASCINATING FACT
The mosquitoes of Lambarda Province are so large and vicious that several years ago the CIA considered recruiting them for a bio-weapons programme.

Note *The drug trade is such an entrenched part of life that local radio stations regularly broadcast trafficking reports.*

Construction work along much of Lambarda's coastline is proceeding at such a rate that swimmers are advised to wear both sunscreen and a hard hat. For additional safety, always swim between the cranes.

Most visitors head for the bustling **beachfront** city of Aguazura but there are many other centres well worth checking out. The former **fishing village** of Nuevo Yelap has become enormously popular with **surfers**, lured by its clean, white beaches, excellent shore breaks and relaxed attitudes towards public drug use. For those on a budget, the southern **settlement** of Puerto Iguna has everything you could ask for in a beach resort, except for a beach and a **resort**. Meanwhile, offshore you'll find dozens of coral caves – tiny islets of white sand and mangroves, inhabited only by **frigate birds** and disgruntled time-share resort owners.

Many of Lambarda's more popular beaches get so crowded that patches of sand must be reserved up to a year in advance.

It is traditional for Lambardan women to wear their first bikini well into their 20s.

Local triathlons involve running, swimming and dismantling the nearest pier.

Aguazura

Built as a shipping port for **coffee** during the boom of the late 18th century, Aguazura began life as a tawdry, **sweltering**, dilapidated place. But a surge of interest in the town as a tourist destination has seen it grow rapidly into a **vibrant**, cosmopolitan resort centre. Known officially as the birthplace of the bikini thong, Aguazura attracts beach-lovers, backpackers, party animals, surfers and sandflies in large numbers. Its warm, **nutrient-rich** waters also attract prodigious numbers of marine animals along with **Venezuelan fishing fleets**, which come year round to plunder the ever-dwindling stocks.

Of course, following such rapid development the city is not without its problems, the major one being pollution. During the **rainy season** everything from **plastic bags** and broken glass to dead squirrels and former members of witness protection schemes gets washed off the streets and into the ocean. Oil spills, too, have marred parts of Aguazura's **pristine coastline** although the ever-inventive locals have capitalised on these frequent **spillages** by building a small refinery on the beach to mop up, and then re-process, petroleum products as they wash ashore.

Aguazura boasts some of the most active (and aggressive) hawkers in Central America. Said to be able to smell a Western wallet from 500m away, these eager entrepreneurs patrol the beach in such numbers that there is simply no need to go shopping in Aguazura – just lie on the sand and a string of goods will be brought to you, everything from trinkets to automotive parts.

Uniformed 'Beach Police' are trained to protect beach-goers and, if necessary, provide massage or hair braiding.

While Aguazura parties 365 days of the year, September is hurricane month and, despite **half-price accommodation** offers, travellers should be wary about visiting the city during this month. Just last year Hurricane **Enrique** battered the coast with ferocious wind and **torrential rain**. At one point 10,000 poorer residents were forcibly evacuated from the city's low lying slum area and forced to act as human sandbags to protect several up-market resorts.

While life guards are posted at most of Lambarda's beaches, swimmers should be aware that they frequently take time off for lunch, siestas, public holidays, religious festivals and to go fishing. Where possible, try and restrict your rescue requirements to outside of these periods.

History

The earliest signs of human **habitation** around Aguazura date from about 6000 BC, in the form of simple **pottery**. These relics are quite crude (literally – most of the specimens found have been ceramic penises) and are believed to belong to the Tz'xuls people, a **primitive** tribe of coastal dwellers who survived by eating shells and driftwood.

In 1505 Spanish naval officier Julio Esquelle was sent to explore the **eastern** coast of San Sombrèro when he spotted a natural **harbour** ringed by fertile land. On 5 April Esquelle stepped ashore with great pomp and ceremony, wearing a velvet coat and brightly **plumed hat**, to officially claim the new land for Spain. However, halfway through his declaration of **sovereignty**, tragedy struck when a large **parrot** – mistaking the feathered headwear for a female companion – swooped, carrying the **diminutive** Spaniard off into the jungle.

Despite Aguazura's isolation from the **capital**, over the years the city has played an important part in San Sombrèro's political history, with some of the country's most deranged **coup leaders** having been born here.

Following a period of decline in the early 20th century, Aguazura underwent something of a resurgence during the 1950s when the beach **resort** became famous for its glamorous **nightlife**, with music, cocktails, prostitutes and gambling attracting a steady stream of visitors, including Mafiosi, film stars and **holidaying** US congressmen.

Traveller's Tip

During the February to March off-season hotel rates can drop 50%, sometimes more. You may, however, find that many of the hotel's facilities are closed and staff absent. In extreme cases, the power and gas will be switched off but for guests prepared to self-cater, the bargains are excellent.

Blessed with a natural harbour, by the 17th century, Aguazura had developed into a major port, catering to visiting sailors with an infrastructure of brothels, taverns and gambling houses. Many of these businesses still operate today, catering to foreign cruise liners and European sporting teams on end-of-season trips.

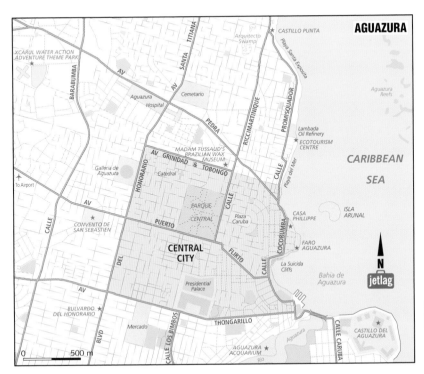

Despite steep harbour walls and canons, the impressive Castillo del Aguazura was ransacked on no fewer than 76 occasions, the attacks only stopping in 1562 when it was decided to point the cannons inland from where the invaders had, most frequently, been approaching.

Where to Stay

There's definitely no shortage of places to stay in Aguazura, with new **hotels** and units going up just as quickly as the planning permits can be improperly obtained. Here, one can find **beachside** accommodation, ranging from exclusive six-star resorts with rooms featuring whirlpool baths so large that **life jackets** are required, through to the most basic of **bures**. As always, you get what you pay for so don't expect too many mod-cons at the budget end. Most rooms will have **ceiling fans** but, more often than not, guests will be required to turn these by hand.

Many of Aguazura's larger resorts offer **poolside activities** and evening 'animations', the San Sombrèran phrase for audience-participation entertainment such as dance contests, **charades** and helping to clean the pool. Whilst taking part is not technically compulsory, guests refusing to join in have reported being **subjected** to uncomfortable levels of verbal and physical intimidation. Be warned.

Weather Warning *During summer the entire coastline of Lambarda is at risk of being hit by hurricanes. In the event of an extreme weather occurence guests will be issued clear instructions by hotel staff, either verbally or in the form of a hastily written note pinned to the front desk moments before it is abandoned.*

🌀🌀🌀 Luxury

✉ *88 Calle Promisquador*
☎ *12 687 695*
@ *playa@palace.com.ss*
▢ *V MC*

Playa Palace Considered one of the region's ultimate resorts, this luxurious enclave is so close to the beach that during unusually high tides its conference room becomes a wave pool. There's an extensive list of activities on offer, including jet-skis, jet-boats and even jets (the Palace boasts its own decommissioned MIG fighter).

✉ *563 Calle Cocorumba*
☎ *12 879 587*
@ *clubmedico@san.com.au*
▢ *V MC DC*

Club Tropicornia Another exclusive resort option, guests arriving at the 'Trop' will be greeted by the property's original native owners who come out in traditional dress – as kitchen hands – and perform a welcome dance. Rooms are, not surprisingly, large and luxurious while the service is impeccable, with lovely touches such as the complimentary turn-down service in which a Swiss watch and chocolate are left on your pillow each night.

Isla Corallina Built on an artificial island just off the coast, this luxurious getaway is popular with movie stars and musicians. (It's main beach is where Keith Richards once fell out of a palm tree – fortunately landing on his head.) Non-guests are kept out by discretely landscaped razor wire fences and the beach is kept so private by hotel security that even the local fish population require I.D. tags. The resort's signature restaurant is *Frutti de Mare*, which, as it's name suggests, serves exclusively horse-meat.

✉ *Isla Arunal*
☎ *12 881 792*
@ *isla@arunal.com.ss*
▭ *DC*

Hotel Luna Beachfront bliss at its very best, the Luna is in a class (and price bracket!) of its very own. Boasting a distinct native theme, each evening at dusk young men will appear in traditional costume, singing and beating a *mali* (junior member of the housekeeping staff) while dancing a thanksgiving ceremony heralding the start of Happy Hour.

✉ *2 Calle Cocorumba*
☎ *12 254 966*
@ *luna@hotel.com.ss*
▭ *V MC*

Traveller's Tip

While many of Aguazura's resorts offer massage treatments, be warned that in some of the cheaper establishments the so-called 'essential oils' used are, in fact, low-grade engine lubricants. Those with sensitive skin or an aversion to being covered in petrochemical by-products should exercise caution.

☁☁ Mid-Range

✉ *89 Av Pedra*
☎ *12 335 468*
@ *mo@lambarda.com.ss*
   pool

Mocambo Surprisingly close to the beach, the reasonably priced Mocambo has a pool, air-conditioned rooms and 'indirect' sea views (you can glimpse water reflected in the windows of a neighbouring hotel block).

✉ *452 Blvd Santa Titiana*
☎ *12 578 744*
@ *moranga@playa.com.ss*
▤ *MC*

Playa Moranga Another less expensive resort option, the Moranga is set back several blocks from the beach but, with favourable winds, it is still possible to smell the rotting seaweed.

✉ *946 Av Thongarillo*
☎ *12 967 413*
@ *sanmarco@hotel.com.ss*
▤ *V MC DC*
   cocktail bar
   rooftop pool
   sauna
   fitness centre

Hotel San Marco Originally a one-star establishment, the San Marco was recently upgraded into a boutique hotel. A rooftop pool, cocktail bar, sauna and fitness centre are all amongst the features listed on the hotel's website but few of these would appear to actually exist anywhere other than in cyberspace. (*Note: The San Marco does offer a Happy Hour but, as this is scheduled between the hours of 8am and 9am, only the most budget-conscious of drinkers are likely to take advantage.*)

✉ *45 Calle Riccimartinique*
☎ *12 963 754*
@ *amore@ricci.com.ss*
▤ *MC*

Playa D'Amor Still popular, this moderately priced beach resort is popular with single men who come for its cheap bars and tawdry strip clubs. The hotel's most notorious feature is its 'turn-down' service that involves a maid being left on your pillow.

Traveller's Tip

Many resorts in Aguazura offer a range of hair and beauty treatments, such as waxing and 'temporary' tattoos. While the latter are advertised as lasting just two weeks, be warned that the accompanying skin lesions often take several months to fully heal.

A typical Aguazura hotel room will generally feature a bible and a TV boasting six channels of 'adult entertainment'. Both can be viewed at the rate of $14.50 per day.

☕ Budget

El Mirador A large, comfortable hotel, the Mirador opened in 2001, on top of a cliff overlooking the main beach. As a result of a minor earthquake the following year, the hotel is now situated at the base of this cliff, somewhat the worse for wear but just as inhabitable.

✉ *5 Calle Caruba*
☎ *12 087 210*
@ *view@mirador.com.ss*

Hacienda Lucia A good value option set several blocks back from the beach. Rooms are all bright (thanks to a lack of curtains) and the hotel boasts three pools, although during peak periods one of these is often used by the hotel laundry to soak soiled tablecloths.

✉ *967 Calle Barabumba*
☎ *12 972 659*
@ *lucia@hacienda.com.ss*
▤ *DC*

Hostel Aguazura The good news is the owner here is friendly and speaks English. The bad news – he snores and you'll be sharing a dorm with him.

✉ *98 Calle Los Bimbos*
☎ *12 669 785*

Hotel Costeria Another popular budget option, the Costeria is clean and quiet, especially on weekends when all facilities appear to shut down for 48 hours. The superior rooms all have views of the ocean while the cheaper standard rooms boast large posters of typical beach scenes.

✉ *97 Av Puerto Flirto*
☎ *12 443 165*
@ *cost@lambarda.com.ss*

Beaches outside Aguazura's up-market resorts are swept each afternoon by staff on behalf of guests who may have lost jewellery, watches, cash or small children during the day.

Where to Eat

Since a lot of resorts in Aguazura are all-inclusive, most **folks** end up eating at their hotel. In fact, many have no choice as the **gates** are locked during meal time and no-one is allowed out until they have had at least three courses and an overpriced cocktail at the **piano bar**.

As a rule it's worth paying a little extra to enjoy a decent **outlook**, especially at night when the twinkling **lights** of ships and steady stream of emergency maritime flares from distressed fishing boats create a truly **romantic** vista.

🌢🌢🌢 Expensive

✉ *64 Calle Cocorumba* ☎ *12 704 814* ▭ *V MC DC*	**Acropolis** On a low cliff overlooking the bay, this stylish restaurant offers sublime San Sombrèran food with an New York twist (a 17.5% service charge). Signature dishes include lobster served in a coconut shell or, if preferred, coconut served in a lobster shell.
✉ *798 Blvd Del Honorario* ☎ *12 975 846* ▭ *V MC*	**Santa Medina** Another top-end eatery, the Medina specialises in seafood and boasts a large aquarium where diners may point at their preferred meal. Accuracy is important or you could end up being served a piece of fake coral or plastic anchor.
✉ *87 Calle Caruba* ☎ *12 611 543* @ *cabana@caruba.com.ss* ▭ *V MC*	**La Cabana** Overlooking the twinkling harbour lights, the Cabana is one of the most romantic restaurants in town. Pleasant touches include colourful prints and ornate native carvings. Unpleasant touches come from the maître d whose fondness for 'da ladeez' borders on sexual harassment.

Corey Writes...
For the Adventure Traveller

The latest craze to hit the Lambarda coast would have to be Surf-Wave Kite-Board Tubing. It's an absolute blast. First, you climb to the top of a cliff and get strapped into a specially designed harness. Then you wake up from a medically induced coma several weeks later in the intensive care ward of Aguazura hospital.

✍️✍️ Mid-Range

Los Dorados This casual yet elegant eatery is housed in an old building that recreates the atmosphere of a typical San Sombrèran home, right down to the heated arguments emanating from its kitchen. An extensive menu features fish and meat, accompanied by a welcome array of green vegetables, along with several somewhat off-putting blue ones.

✉ *348 Calle Riccimartinique*
☎ *12 975 014*
▤ *MC*

Casa Casa Local dishes include *pollo criollo*, yam and spiced swordfish. There is also a 'Menu Americano', featuring the same dishes served double sized and with fries.

✉ *873 Av Thongarillo*
☎ *12 367 940*
@ *casa@casa.com.au*
▤ *V MC*

La Rosticeria Loud background music sets a groovy ambience and just about drowns out the sound of other diners groaning with gastric distress. Of an evening the mosquitoes tend to be a little annoying, as are the roving violinists, but both can be repelled with aerosol spray.

✉ *56 Av Grinidad & Tobongo*
☎ *12 701 497*
@ *groovy@rosticeria.com.ss*
▤ *V*

✍️ Budget

La Marina Describing itself as a 'seaside eatery' (despite being several kilometres inland), the Marina carries this theme through with a range of maritime memorabilia such as nets, anchors and lobster pots adorning the dining room and a permanent oil slick emerging from the kitchen.

✉ *9780 Calle Barabumba*
☎ *12 310 255*
@ *sea@lamarina.com.ss*

El Senorio Whilst cheap and pleasant, this open-fronted restaurant is on the main road through town and, as a consequence, suffers greatly from traffic fumes. This, along with the fact that 90% of the staff and customers smoke, means that El Senorio is not recommended for anyone with a respiratory disorder or an aversion to developing one.

✉ *27 Av Puerto Flirto*
☎ *12 975 358*

For a taste of authentic Aguazuran cuisine, try visiting a pousana, *or beach-front café. Food here is served in the traditional style: two hours after it has been ordered, cold and to the wrong table.*

Of course, it's not all sun, surf and hedonistic pleasure in Aguazura, the city also boasts many cultural attractions such as its prestigious Art Gallery. Walking anti-clockwise round its many exhibition rooms takes you through the entire sweep of local art, starting with the pre-Columbian era and ending with the public toilets.

Attractions

While most visitors come to Aguazura for its splendid **beaches** and water-based activities, there are many other attractions to enjoy in and around the city.

PARQUE CENTRAL An **oasis** of green in the centre of town, this shady **square** is dominated by a statue of Hermano Pedra, the city's famous freedom fighter. Visitors will often comment on how lifelike this **statue** appears, almost as if Hermano himself had been covered in **bronze**. He was.

HACIENDA FELIPEZ One of the city's oldest building, this was the original residence of its first **governor**, Jorje Felipez. The house was strategically placed to face east so that the first floor windows looked out over the bay. A **canon** is still trained out of the bedroom window, in readiness for pirate ships or door-to-door **salesmen**. A statue of Governor Felipez about to **mount** his steed once stood out front but has been removed on the grounds of obscenity.

CASTILLO PUNTA Another of the city's original buildings, this aristocratic residence was built on **coastal swampland** in 1678. Originally a four-storey **building**, now just a single floor pokes above ground, the bottom three buried – along with its **architect** – beneath the sodden ground.

Bulavardo del Honorario For those interested in local government, this **stretch** of pavement commemorates each of the town's previous governors with a **star** marking the exact spot where they were **gunned** down.

AGUAZURA AGUARIO Built just a few years ago, this aquarium has one of the largest displays of fresh- and **saltwater fish** in Latin America. Of particular note is the giant sea turtle (*galapago grande)* display that evocatively depicts the **life cycle** of these magnificent creatures, from eggs to nori rolls.

FARO AGUAZURA This historic lighthouse has stood sentinel over the harbour for centuries. Visitors are welcome to climb the tower for a **bird's-eye view** of the city, provided they **promise** not to touch the switch marked 'off'.

THE ESCOBAR WATER ACTION ADVENTURE THEME PARK is, despite its promising name, little more than a flooded quarry on the edge of town with a few car tyres dangling from ropes above the **murky abyss**. (In fact, 'The Murky Abyss' is one of the park's feature attractions.)

HOLY DROP!

To the east of the city centre you'll find the Convento de Santa Sebastien. This impressive monastery is home to the Sebastienite Monks, an ancient order founded, for tax purposes, in 1578. Here, monks manufacture the mysterious herbal liqueur, *Agua de Dios.* According to legend, the formula for *Agua de Dios.* was invented by a 16th-century alchemist who was attempting to create *acqua vitae*, or the waters of life. While his original brew fell somewhat short of this miraculous goal, it did prove an excellent all-purpose stain remover and, following subsequent refinements, led to the creation of a curiously pleasing tonic. In 1598 the formula for *Agua de Dios.* was bequeathed to the order who have overseen its production ever since. The precise recipe, involving 120 herbs, has always been a closely guarded secret, although a recent case brought before court by Jewish drinkers has forced manufacturers to admit that at least one of the 120 herbs is, in fact, pork.

Diving

The magnificent **reefs** off Aguazura have sadly suffered from severe bleaching in recent years, meaning that many sections are now a dull shade of grey. However, vivd reds and oranges can still be found, usually where **rusted car bodies** have been dumped. Various operators offer trips out to the reef. In addition, some beach resorts permit non-certified divers to use scuba equipment, provided they go no deeper than 5m and agree to help clean the pool.

Swimming

Despite its idyllic looks, stretches of beach near Aguazura can be treacherous. There are **strong rip-tides**, and deaths frequently occur, often the result of swimmers who have got into trouble in the water being fought over by eager life guards all keen to claim a cash bonus for rescuing them.

Chillin' Out

The closest beach to Aguazura is Playa Comunal. One of the city's most crowded and polluted stretches of shoreline, it's also home to the **Ecotourism Centre**. Touts offering everything from **massages** to minor medical procedures continue to be a problem here although it is possible to pay a tout to keep other touts at bay.

DEATH DEFYING DIVERS

Aguazura's famed cliff divers plunge some 35m from the cliffs of La Suicida into a tight, rocky channel, timing their leap to coincide with an incoming wave of paying tourists. Unfortunately, by the end of each day these brave athletes often have so many coins stuffed in their swimming trunks that they will sink to the bottom without trace.

Music is such a part of life in Lambarda that even shark warnings are delivered to beach-goers in the form of song.

Whale watching

Humpback whales visit the **calving grounds** off Aguazura in large numbers during the March–May period. These majestic animals are easy to spot from the shore – just look for the fleet of Japanese 'research' boats chasing them. Whilst the whales can be viewed from the shore, many prefer to take a **boat** out for a closer look. Strict regulations prohibit craft coming within 500m of any whale although some renegade operators clearly flaunt this law. One in particular, *Barnacle Bob*, offers customers the opportunity to 'carve your name in their blubber'. Do not support this company.

Fishing

The waters off Aguazura are rich in nutrients, largely as a result of **cruise ships** pumping out their bilge contents as they pass by. Keen anglers can try their hand at deep sea sportfishing for marlin, sailfish, tuna and San Sombrèro's most prized trophy, the guava shark. Considered one of the most aggressive of all saltwater species, this shark has been known to **attack** its own tail during frenzied feeding displays. The International Game Fishing record for a guava shark stands at 73kg. Last year a local angler claimed to have landed a 76kg monster but this could never be authenticated because the shark ate the **scales**, before escaping back over the side of the boat.

Helena Writes...

For the Eco-Traveller

On a recent whale-watching trip off the coast of Lambarda we caught a glimpse of a pod of Alaskan greys. Unfortunately, some of my fellow passengers began taking photos, not realising that the electronic motor drives of their cameras could interfere with the whale's sensitive sonar systems. I had to capsize the rubber dinghy in order to prevent a potential ecological disaster.

Aguazura's Dr Roman performs beach-side massages as well as minor cosmetic surgery.

06 San Sombrèro
MARACCA PROVINCE

Maracca Province

Few regions conjure up more **evocative** images in the imaginations of travellers than the **rainforests** of Maracca. Dense **jungle**, abundant wildlife and indigenous tribes so cut off from the modern world that many are yet to get **broadband internet** services make this a destination of mythical proportions.

A once heavily forested region, Maracca Province is now made up of almost a dozen separate national parks, including the extensive **Quintara Parque Nacional**, scene of heated protest activity in 2002 when **environmental** groups failed to stop a gas pipeline being built through this **fragile wilderness zone**. They were, however, successful in having the pipe painted green.

The Maraccan rainforest boasts an incredible 3000 separate species of **wildlife** and, while 90% of these are actually tarantulas, the level of **biodiversity** is remarkable.

One of the best ways to appreciate the Maraccan rainforest is via a **canopy walk**. These purpose-built platforms allow visitors to experience a **bird's-eye view** of the jungle canopy without damaging its delicate **ecosystems**. Sadly, some less than scrupulous tour operators will offer to simply chop down a section of forest for you, but these services should be avoided.

HEALTH

According to Maracca's Chief Health Officer, malaria has been largely eradicated from the province. But his death, some weeks after this pronouncement, from 'a head cold' has caused many to question its veracity.

Helena Writes...

For the Eco-Traveller
When hiring a guide, I always try to find a local one with a good reputation who works in harmony with the indigenous community. Then I offer to marry him.

Many visitors to Maracca make the pre-dawn ascent up Mount Ibrazu to watch the sun appear over its summit. While this event is typically obscured by thick cloud, most tour guides carry extensive photo albums of previous sunrises.

In addition to its rainforests, two other natural features define Maracca Province. The first is the mighty Rio Pongo, which carves its way through the region's **densest jungles**. A cruise on the Pongo is highly **recommended** although visitors heading up-river are advised to ask for a seat on the left-hand side of the boat; the scenery is no better but you're less likely to be hit by a native blow-dart. The other dominant feature is, of course, the towering **Volcan Ismeralda**, one of the largest active volcanoes in all of Central America. This rumbling **edifice** was climbed in 1704 by Spanish mountaineer Diegos Cuervez who, struck by the volcano's size and constant belching of **foul gasses**, named it after his wife Ismeralda.

Maracca Province offers a range of exciting options for the adventurous visitor. (Clockwise from top) **Agritourism** *– stay in actual farmhouses (hovellos) with typical rural families.* **Ecotourism** *– live with indigenous locals in authentic village surroundings.* **Militourism** *– this exciting new 'Embedded & Breakfast' scheme allows visitors to spend several days holed up with a variety of militia units.*

Wildlife

Many visitors to Maracca come to experience the province's extraordinary range of **wildlife**, including primates, **big cats** and *endentates* (toothless mammals such as anteaters and sugar cane farmers). While illegal **poaching** has taken its toll on many species, the government is fighting back, with the appointment of numerous wildlife officers. These officials can be easily identified by their distinctive **uniforms**, made from the **pelts** of endangered jaguars.

In an effort to attract birdlife depleted by illegal poachers, wooden toucans were recently placed throughout Maracca's jungles. Unfortunately, many of these were subsequently stolen by illegal loggers.

Some of the **exotic** creatures you might be lucky enough to encounter include large flocks of *toucanos monotonos* (drab toucans), the only **colourless** members of this bird species known to exist. Then there are **capybaras**, believed to be the largest rodents in the world. Despite having long, frightening claws as well as a **foul stench**, these fierce creatures feature heavily as characters in children's books and cartoons. The **elusive tamarin lion** exists only in the jungles of Maracca and is so rare that there are believed to be only half a dozen **mating pairs** left, three of which are in travelling circuses.

After almost a century of constant warfare, the bark on many trees in Maraccan rainforests has developed a naturally bullet-holed appearance.

Despite spending much of their life hanging upside down from trees, Maracca's Chuquito Monkeys are, in fact, a surprisingly intelligent species and in 2003 one even made it through the fastest finger first section of Who Wants to Be a Millionaire.

San Pistachio

The capital of Maracca, and stepping-off point for most visitors to the **region**, is the river port township of San Pistachio. Situated on the **muddy banks** of the Rio Pongo, most houses here are built on stilts to escape wet-season **floods** and roving packs of rabid dogs. Not surprisingly, few **travellers** spend much time in San Pistachio, using it merely to organise expeditions **up-river** to the many fascinating villages that can be reached by boat.

WHEN TO GO
Because few travellers visit during the rainy season, you probably won't need reservations. You will, however, need an inflatable dinghy and strong survival instincts.

The other 'must' for visitors to San Pistachio is a torch. Electricity supplies are at best **erratic** and power outages frequent. Local authorities are experimenting with **alternative energy sources**, including hydro-electricity. Sadly, due to deforestation the Rio Pongo is so badly **silted** up that the newly-opened hydro power station has become irreversibly clogged. However, plans to convert this plant into a **mud-powered** facility are being considered. More successful has been the San Pistachio's experiment with **geo-thermal power**. In fact, during periods of intense **seismic** activity it is possible to boil a kettle in under seven seconds.

We Were Wrong. In our last edition it was stated that many visitors to San Pistachio 'fly from Maranao City'. They do, in fact, 'flee from Maranoa City'.

FASCINATING FACT
While many assume the smell of rancid meat that hangs over San Pistachio emanates from the city's tannery, it does, in fact, come from the Hombros Vielle steakhouse (open Tues–Sat).

Where to Stay

Many **native villages** throughout Maracca will take visitors, either as guests or **hostages**, for short stays. During this time you will live, eat, work (and, on occasions, marry) within the community in often the most **basic** of conditions. While no doubt **authentic**, such arrangements may not suit everyone. For those after slightly less austere **accommodation**, consider the following options:

Eco-lodges are going up in Maracca as fast as the surrounding rainforest can be cleared.

Macawa Jungle Lodge

Perfect for those wishing to **experience** the Maraccan rainforest without foregoing too many **home comforts**, the Macawa Lodge offers the ultimate in luxury. Guests arriving at the Macawa are greeted with a cocktail featuring two **umbrellas**, one decorative and the other to shelter you from the inevitable tropical **downpours**, before being ushered into their native-style jungle huts.

The emphasis here is on total relaxation, achieved through a combination of yoga and **rum-based** cocktails. Then there are a series of 'ultimate massages' including one that involves being rubbed down with **truffle oil**. The lodge is eco-conscious (insomuch as they're conscious of the environmental damage the establishment is doing) and boasts an elegant, old-world feel. Spread over several hectares, guests can watch from their balconies as **peacocks**, flamingos and African cranes strut around a landscaped pool, blissfully unaware that several of them are about to become that evening's **casserole**. The lobby shop sells nature-theme T-shirts, cards and posters, and devotes a portion of the **profits** to 'conservation projects' (currently a fund for the owners to purchase a new diesel generator).

Guests at the Macawa Jungle Lodge should take care as there have been several recent reports of people waking from a deep tissue massage treatment to find, not only their clothes and jewellery missing, but also several vital organs.

Pongo Eco-Lodge

One of Maracca's most famous **eco-lodges**, Shakri is a 'green' hotel and relies on low energy lighting (so bring a torch) as well as **recycling** – tonight's bread roll is tomorrow's crouton. Set amidst lush rainforest gardens, the Lodge has charming small rooms and at night one can experience the sounds of nature or, if next door to the **communal bathrooms**, nature calling.

There is a small pond out front that, after heavy rain, often extends in through the front bedrooms, however guests are offered **waterproof slippers** and an identification guide to local **aquatic** species. Each evening there are lectures from wildlife experts that are informative and in depth. They're also in Spanish so it's worth bringing a dictionary.

The Lodge utilises wind power which, while ecologically sound, can be somewhat erratic and guests are advised against using **electrical appliances** such as shavers during **strong gales**. At night you can enjoy looking at the stars using the resort's telescope or – due to frequent low cloud – your own **imagination**. There's also a comfortable dining room where you can relax, read or enjoy a lecture – often provided by fellow guests **disgruntled** at your choice of non-recyclable footwear.

Maracca Health Retreat

For those less concerned with luxury, the Maracca Health Retreat offers an excellent way to unwind in a **pristine** jungle setting. Upon arrival, guests are fitted with **terry-towelling robes** and an electronic bracelet that will sound an alarm should you attempt to abscond. Next comes a consultation with one of the Retreat's **medical** staff. While few are trained doctors, all wear white coats and will conduct a thorough examination of each guest's history, both medical and financial, to determine the most appropriate **treatment** plan. Invariably this will involve mud wraps, mud baths and a high-altitude plunge into a mud pool resulting – more often than not – in a **mud enema**.

A range of therapeutic, if somewhat vigorous, massage treatments are also offered, including the local *purani* style, a form of massage known to **improve blood circulation**, build muscle flexibility and generate oxygen supply. Unfortunately most of these benefits accrue to the person actually performing the treatment.

RAINFOREST SAFARIS

Many travellers come to Maracca expecting to see jaguars behind every tree and spear-toting natives **dancing** around every village. While this sort of thing can be arranged (for a cost), the reality is that catching a glimpse of **monkeys**, birds, bats or reptiles can often prove difficult. Those prepared to **camp** out might be rewarded with a glimpse of (or bite from) something exotic but encountering wildlife is often just a matter of luck and patience. Of course, your best option is to hire a **local guide**. A good one will point out plants, birds and animals you're likely to miss on your own. A poor one will simply use the opportunity to borrow **money** or visit relatives living in distant villages.

On many rainforest treks a local porter will walk ahead with your gear. This is the last time you are ever likely to see him, or it, again.

Trekking – Our experts advise…

Philippe Writes… For the Serious Traveller

Often the only way to reach remote jungle areas is as part of an organised tour. However, this means travelling with other people, potentially diminishing the authenticity of your travel experience. For this reason, whenever I join a trek I inform the other participants that I wish to be left alone and not included in social activities. They are obviously saddened about not having my company, but most manage to conceal their disappointment.

Tina Writes… For the Cautious Traveller

Many so-called 'reputable' trekking companies are little more than fronts for scam artists who will lure you into the rainforest and then make off with your gear. Regardless of how many porters there might be, always insist on carrying your own pack and, where possible, handcuff yourself to the guide.

Corey Writes… For the adventure traveller

One of Maracca's most popular walks is the *Allmeira Circuit,* a route that takes in native villages, spectacular mountain scenery and heaps of exotic wildlife. Doing the 'Allmeira' normally takes two weeks but, since the advent of ultra extreme sprint trekking, it is possible to complete this circuit in under 48 hours, provided you are prepared to travel at night, dispense with meal breaks, by-pass all sites of cultural significance and never let your speed drop below a brisk jog.

Helena Writes… For the Eco-Traveller

Remember, it is not only illegal, but extremely irresponsible, to buy souvenirs that involve the use of wild animals in their production. And don't be fooled by villagers who claim that the animal in question died of 'natural causes'. Three-week-old baby crocodiles do not, as a rule, suffer heart attacks, acute arthritis or dementia.

Index

JETLAG TRAVEL PRESENTS!

Our latest range of Special Interest Tours. Departing soon…

Jocelyn Newbury's GREAT GARDENS OF THE WORLD

Let the irrepressible host of BBC2's *Bloomin' Marvellous* take you on a horticultural cruise.

* Follow the trail of the elm leaf beetle through Europe.
* Marvel at the Arid Gardens of Africa – mulch ado about nothing!
* Visit the world's oldest compost heap.

Price includes airfares, accommodation (arbour or gazebo), meals and cuttings, plus all of Jocelyn's mildly tedious but generally informative anecdotes. What others have said:

'*A most informative and exciting trip. The time spent exploring fibrous root systems of the Mediterranean simply flew by.*'

Golf Heaven

Deregistered former PGA pro Freddie 'Cranky' Wilkes will be your 'caddy' on this once-in-a-lifetime tour.

* **Royal Llleywwwefffllleyyyn!** Triple bogey your way around one of the wettest courses in Wales.
* **Irish Odyssey** Ballybunnion, Royal Carbuncle, Wartsmead and, of course, historic Fungall Downs make up the best that the Emerald Isle has to offer.
* **Royal Dubai** Boasting the largest sand-trap in the world – players landing here will need a pitching wedge and at least three day's worth of provisions.
* **Lochmaggis** Part of Scotland's famed peat belt. One of the few clubs where members may still be executed for wearing incorrect attire.

Price includes air fares, hotels, green fees and constant criticism of your golf swing by Freddy. (Lost balls will also attract a surcharge.)

A Year In…

For those with time to dream, come with us to an untouched part of Europe where we'll help you purchase a derelict farmhouse, renovate the barn, learn to cook like a native, marry a local tradesman and get a book deal, all within the space of 12 months.

JETLAG

The ultimate website for travellers to swap advice, offer tips and ask questions. Learn from those who have been there before!

Author: cherek
Date: 23/03/2006, 3:19 pm
Can anyone suggest an inexpensive but clean hotel in downtown Buenos Aires? I have a two night stopover there this September.

Author: MG
Date: 23/03/2006, 3:40 pm
I've heard the Melia Grande in Tioca is supposed to be good. Large rooms, friendly service and, if you book and pay 30 days in advance, you can take advantage of our additional super-saver accommodation deals.

(Editor – Please, this is a traveller's discussion forum – would commercial operators kindly refrain from using the service for advertising purposes!)

Author: MG
Date: 23/03/2006, 3:41 pm
The Melia Grande – your home away from home.

(Editor – Okay, you're officially banned)

Eager for the latest travel advice? Or just spoiling for a fight that only three people in the world could find remotely interesting?

Author: Jurgen10
Date: 15/02/2006, 3:00 pm
Re. comments on my recent post regarding alpine trekking options, if G.W. had actually read my comments he would have realised that I was not in any way disparaging micro-fibre fabrics as a viable alternative to Gortex, I was merely suggesting that, in certain circumstances, the semi-permeable outer layer may provide greater comfort and durability.

(Editor – As this particular thread has been running for over six months we feel it might be time to end all correspondence on the matter)

Author: GW Climber
Date: 15/02/2006, 3:02 pm
Hang on, we haven't finished yet.

(Editor – Yes you have)

PLUS! Our Travel Chums service. An ideal way for solo travellers to find that perfect partner.

< #17J45B > My name is Jillian, I'm 22. Next year I plan to backpack through Europe and I'm looking for a person to pick up the bills and buy me things.

< #13D22K > Hi, I'm Danny, heading to South America in August–September. Looking for someone to share the trip. Not interested in romance or anything sleazy.

< #10C89A > My name Carlos. I am looking for someone to carry a small suitcase to Central America and then bring it back. Leaving Sept 3, return the following day.

< #13D22K > Hi, Danny again. Just thought I'd clarify something. While I said I'm not looking for romance or anything sleazy I wouldn't actually say 'no' to either. I mean, whatever.

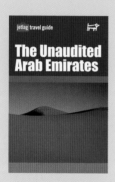

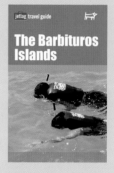

The Unaudited Arab Emirates

This tiny desert republic boasts a population of 3 million people (80% of whom are members of the Royal Family) and is famous for hotels so luxurious that many rooms come with their own individual reception desk. The UAE is a shopper's paradise and no trip would be complete without a visit to the Bedouin markets of Hagul where traditional rugs are sold alongside plasma screens and used BMW's.

Costa Lottsa

This ultra exclusive stretch of coastline between Italy and France remains a legally separate protectorate where residency can only be obtained through birth or by becoming a Formula 1 driver. With more roulette wheels per square kilometre than any other country in the world, it's little wonder that the official currency of Costa Lottsa is the casino chip, while the national dress is the tuxedo.

The Barbituros Islands

Formally known as Grinidad and Tobongo, this is one of the Caribbean's best snorkelling and scuba destinations, diving is so popular here that a recent census classified 3% of the population as officially 'living underwater'.

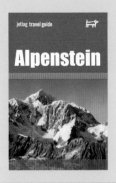

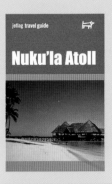

Alpenstein

Tyranistan

Nuku'la Atoll

This tiny European principality is known mostly for its famed twin skiing peaks, Mont Overprix and Mont Blancheque. An alpine haven for the ultra rich and ultra chic, Alpenstein boasts the highest rate of domestic staff in the world, reflected in its three official languages: Italian, French and Filipino. While a shameful affiliation with Nazi Germany is now long behind the country, more than 22% of citizens still list their nationality as 'Aryan Master-race'.

Offcially known as a republic, but more commonly referred to as a 'flashpoint', Tyranistan is famous for being one of the few countries Genghis Khan was too afraid to ever enter. This former Soviet Republic still retains close ties to Russia, as more than 60% of the Kremlin's nuclear waste is currently stored here. Birthplace of the balaclava, Tyranistan has something to offer everyone, from its exotic capital Vladivodka to the remote yellow-topped Urinal Mountains.

Home to the Polystyroneasian people, this remote Pacific archipelago continues to draw visitors with its collection of eerie stone statues, many of which stand more than three metres high, four if you count the advertising hoardings now mounted on top. A former French colony, the influence of France can still be felt in the island's language, cuisine and disturbingly high radioactivity levels.

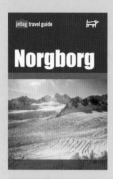

Norgborg – Artic Jewel

Perched precariously high above the Artic Circle, the ice-encrusted island of Norgborg may be cold but it's fast becoming one of Europe's hottest destinations! Nature is the big attraction here and, for the warmly-dressed visitor, there's so much to see. Take a bracingly therapeutic dip in the ice baths of Limpkoch. Lose yourself on a windswept tundra so vast that it's possible to travel for hours without seeing an oil-drilling platform. Or head for the coast to catch a glimpse of majestic humpback whales in their natural environment (the refrigerated hold of a Japanese trawler). And, when you've had enough of the wildlife, check out the nightlife in the capital city Volvhagaan where you can watch scantily-clad llapland dancers strutting their stuff in fur bikinis.

Full Country Name: Norgborg (Norgbourg) or Fakse Lademan (local name)
Area: 156 square kilometres (or less, depending on global warming)
Population: 15,050
Capital City: Volvhaagan
People: 86% Norborger, 14% sea-lion
Language: Nuknuk
Religion: 92% Evangelical Lutheran, 7% Roman Catholic and 3 followers of Benny Hin
Government: Autocratic Theocracy
Head of State: Queen Bjork II
Major Industries: Fishing, aquaculture, oil and storing Uzbekistan's unwanted nuclear waste
Staple Diet: Krill
Entry Requirements: Vaccinations are not required but visitors must hold a valid passport and at least seven day's worth of thermal underwear

Other Places to Visit
Jamtaart, Laaga, Brestfheeden, Limpkoch, Kunsbac, Nooneholm, Ringhurten and Bjornborg.

FASCINATING FACT…
The world's first ever ice hotel opened in Norgborg in 1993 when the heating system at the Holiday Inn broke down.

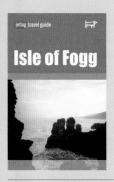

Isle of Fogg – Destination Drizzle

Of the 23 land masses that make up the remote Outcropp Islands, only the Isle of Fogg is inhabited by humans. It's a stunning place of craggy headlands, wild surf-drenched beaches and moor lands so desolate that many of the sheep grazing here require anti-depressant medication. Don't be put off by the bracing wind and almost constant drizzle, as there's plenty to enjoy inside, such as the impressive Kelp Museum, the only three-storey building in the world to have been constructed entirely out of driftwood. Nature lovers, too, will inevitably be drawn by the thousands of sea kites who pass over the island. While spotting these drab birds in the low cloud can be a challenge, it is easy to marvel at their colourful droppings.

Whether you're being buffeted by gales or beaten with a fragrant branch of birch leaves at a local sauna, a visit to Fogg will stay with you long after the effects of hypothermia have worn off.

Full Country Name: The British Protectorate of Fogg
Capital city: Bogg
People: Predominantly Scottish, along with a few Danes and a former Taliban chief
Language: Loud English (so as to be heard above the wind)
Religion: Knitting
Head of State: King Orrstrum the Buffeted (he also runs the Post Office)
Major Industries: fishing, wool, piracy

Other Places to Visit
Misst, Cloddnonn Hoare, Peatlik, Mt. Guano, Brrrrrh, Gusebumhp and Bahnicle.

FASCINATING FACT…
The Isle of Fogg was actually visited in 1872 by Charles Darwin who, after observing the local people, came very close to abandoning his theory of evolution.

The Jetlag Story

The story begins in 1978 when three friends, Santo Cilauro, Tom Gleisner and Rob Sitch (left) spent a year travelling through Southeast Asia and Europe. Disappointed with the lack of decent guidebooks available to young travellers, they decided to write one themselves, undertaking extensive research during the course of their trip. Upon returning home, however, the boys discovered that all they had were a few notes scrawled on the back of beer coasters, along with the phone number of a waitress in Manchester and a photo of some hills.

Despite this lack of solid source material, the three set about producing their first book, hand-typing, editing, stapling and even proofreading the manuscript themselves. *Europe on a Shostring* proved to be an instant hit, its first print run selling out within days (there were, admittedly, just three copies), and marking the birth of an exciting new player on the travel book scene.

Since then Jetlag has gone on to publish over 100 separate titles, including guidebooks, phrasebooks, activity guides, maps, newsletters and a popular collection of erotic travel stories.

While Jetlag Publishing is now a multinational enterprise, employing close to 300 staff around the world, Santo, Tom and Rob's ethos has always remained the same: all profits go to them.